MENTAL MODEL

THE BEST PRODUCTIVE,PROFITABLE AND POSITIVE TIPS IN
WORK, IN LIFE, AND IN THE FAMILY. THE ART OF THINKING
BEFORE ACTING

By

Jack Collins

Contents

INTRODUCTION

Mental models are deeply ingrained assumptions or generalizations that influence how we understand the world and how we take action. Some other words we use for mental models are perspectives, beliefs, assumptions, and mind set, to name a few. Mental models are often the greatest barriers to implementing new ideas in organizations, but they are also the area of organizational learning where organizations can make the most significant impact.

Unfortunately, assumptions, the word most often used to refer to mental models, have a negative connotation to most of us. We've all heard the old adage, "You know what happens when you assume? It makes an ___ out of you and me." Well, you can fill in the blank. Assumptions, nonetheless, are the only way we can make sense of our complex world. It is not possible to have complete information about every situation we encounter, so by their very nature, our assumptions or mental models are incomplete and therefore flawed. For the most part, however, our mental models serve us well.

There are those occasions, on the other hand, where our mental models lead us astray. A great example of how imperfect mental models can be comes from the ancient parable of the blind men and the elephant, where several blind men are feeling different parts of an elephant and describing it. The descriptions by themselves are inaccurate, but when combined into one, give a clearer albeit still flawed description of what an elephant really looks like. Mental models are like puzzle pieces that we need to fit together into a larger whole. As different mental models are recognized, another piece falls in to place, and we see a clearer picture, but in this work, we do not have the top of the puzzle box to guide us. We must grope along like the blind men.

Mental models affect what we see in situations and create reinforcing patterns of behavior.

What are mental models?

Mental models are psychological representations of real, hypothetical, or imaginary situations. They were first postulated by the American philosopher Charles Sanders Peirce, who postulated (1896) that reasoning is a process by which a human "examines the state of things asserted in the premisses, forms a diagram of that state of things, perceives in the parts of the diagram relations not explicitly mentioned in the premisses, satisfies itself by mental experiments upon the diagram that these relations would always subsist, or at least would do so in a certain proportion of cases, and concludes their necessary, or probable, truth."

The Scottish psychologist Kenneth Craik (1943) proposed a similar idea; he believed that the mind constructs "small-scale models" of reality that it uses to anticipate events, to reason, and to underlie explanation. Like pictures in Wittgenstein's (1922) "picture" theory of the meaning of language, mental models have a structure that corresponds to the structure of what they represent. They are accordingly akin to architects' models of buildings, to molecular biologists' models of complex molecules, and to physicists' diagrams of particle interactions.

Since Craik's insight, cognitive scientists have argued that the mind constructs mental models as a result of perception, imagination and knowledge, and the comprehension of discourse. They study how children develop such models, how to design artifacts and computer systems for which it is easy to acquire a model, how a model of one domain may serve as analogy for another domain, and how models engender thoughts, inferences, and feelings.

How we reason

The theory of mental models rests on simple principles, and it extends in a natural way to inferring probabilities, to decision making, and to recursive reasoning about other people's reasoning. We can summarize the theory in terms of its principal predictions, which have all been corroborated experimentally. According to the model theory, everyday reasoning depends on the simulation of events in mental models (e.g., Johnson-Laird, 2006). The principal assumptions of the theory are:

- Each model represents a possibility. Its structure corresponds to the structure of the world, but it has symbols for negation, probability, believability, and so on. Models that are kinematic or dynamic unfold in time to represent sequences of events.
- Models are iconic insofar as possible, that is, their parts and relations correspond to those of the situations that they represent. They underlie visual images, but they also represent abstractions, and so they can represent the extensions of all sorts of relations. They can also be supplemented by symbolic elements to represent, for example, negation.
- Models explain deduction, induction, and explanation. In a valid deduction, the conclusion holds for all models of the premises.

In an induction, knowledge eliminates models of possibilities, and so the conclusion goes beyond the information given. In an abduction, knowledge introduces new concepts in order to yield an explanation.

- The theory gives a 'dual process' account of reasoning. System 1 constructs initial models of premises and is restricted in computational power, i.e., it cannot carry out recursive inferences. System 2 can follow up the consequences of consequences recursively, and therefore search for counterexamples, where a counterexample is a model of the premises in which the conclusion does not hold.

- The greater the number of alternative models needed, the harder it is: we take longer and are more likely to err, especially by overlooking a possibility. In the simulation of a sequence of events, the later in the sequence that a critical event occurs, the longer it will take us to make the inference about it.

- The principle of truth: mental models represent only what is true, and accordingly they predict the occurrence of systematic and compelling fallacies if inferences depend on what is false. An analogous principle applies to the representation of what is possible rather than impossible, to what is permissible rather than impermissible, and to other similar contrasts.

- The meanings of terms such as 'if' can be modulated by content and knowledge. For example, our geographical knowledge modulates the disjunction: Jay is in Stockholm or he is in Sweden. Unlike most disjunctions, this one yields a definite conclusion: Jay is in Sweden.

The theory accounts for the informality of arguments in science and daily life, whereas logic is notoriously of little help in analyzing them. If people base such arguments on mental models, then there is no reason to suppose that they will lay them out like the steps of a formal proof. The theory of mental models, however, is not a paragon. It is radically incomplete; and it is likely to have problems and deficiencies. Proponents of rule theories have accused it of every conceivable shortcoming from blatant falsehood to untestability. It postulates that human reasoners can in principle see the force of counterexamples, and indeed people are able to construct them — a competence that is beyond the power of formal rule theories to explain. The model theory may well be overturned by counterexamples predicted by a superior theory. In which case, it will at least have had the virtue of accounting for its own demise.

The Secret to Great Thinking and Decision Making

Expanding your set of mental models is something experts need to work on just as much as novices. We all have our favorite mental models, the ones we naturally default to as an explanation for how or why something happened. As you grow older and develop expertise in a certain area, you tend to favor the mental models that are most familiar to you.

Here's the problem: when a certain worldview dominates your thinking, you'll try to explain every problem you face through that worldview. This pitfall is particularly easy to slip into when you're smart or talented in a given area.

The more you master a single mental model, the more likely it becomes that this mental model will be your downfall because you'll start applying it indiscriminately to every problem. What looks like expertise is often a limitation. As the common proverb says, "If all you have is a hammer, everything looks like a nail."

When a certain worldview dominates your thinking, you'll try to explain every problem you face through that worldview.

Consider this example from biologist Robert Sapolsky. He asks, "Why did the chicken cross the road?" Then, he provides answers from different experts.

- If you ask an evolutionary biologist, they might say, "The chicken crossed the road because they saw a potential mate on the other side."
- If you ask a kinesiologist, they might say, "The chicken crossed the road because the muscles in the leg contracted and pulled the leg bone forward during each step."
- If you ask a neuroscientist, they might say, "The chicken crossed the road because the neurons in the chicken's brain fired and triggered the movement."

Technically speaking, none of these experts are wrong. But nobody is seeing the entire picture either. Each individual mental model is just one view of reality. The challenges and situations we face in life cannot be entirely explained by one field or industry.

All perspectives hold some truth. None of them contain the complete truth.

Relying on a narrow set of thinking tools is like wearing a mental straitjacket. Your cognitive range of motion is limited. When your set of mental models is limited, so is your potential for finding a solution. In order to unleash your full potential, you have to collect a range of mental models. You have to build out your decision making toolbox.

Thus, the secret to great thinking is to learn and employ a variety of mental models.

Expanding Your Set of Mental Models

The process of accumulating mental models is somewhat like improving your vision. Each eye can see something on its own. But if you cover one of them, you lose part of the scene. It's impossible to see the full picture when you're only looking through one eye.

Similarly, mental models provide an internal picture of how the world works. We should continuously upgrade and improve the quality of this picture. This means reading widely from the best books, studying the fundamentals of seemingly unrelated fields, and learning from people with wildly different life experiences.

The mind's eye needs a variety of mental models to piece together a complete picture of how the world works. The more sources you have to draw upon, the clearer your thinking becomes. As the philosopher Alain de Botton notes, "The chief enemy of good decisions is a lack of sufficient perspectives on a problem."

The Pursuit of Liquid Knowledge

In school, we tend to separate knowledge into different silos— biology, economics, history, physics, philosophy. In the real world, information is rarely divided into neatly defined categories. In the words of Charlie Munger, "All the wisdom of the world is not to be found in one little academic department."

World-class thinkers are often silo-free thinkers. They avoid looking at life through the lens of one subject. Instead, they develop "liquid knowledge" that flows easily from one topic to the next.

This is why it is important to not only learn new mental models, but to consider how they connect with one another. Creativity and innovation often arise at the intersection of ideas. By spotting the links between various mental models, you can identify solutions that most people overlook.

Here's the good news:

You don't need to master every detail of every subject to become a world-class thinker. Of all the mental models humankind has generated throughout history, there are just a few dozen that you need to learn to have a firm grasp of how the world works.

Many of the most important mental models are the big ideas from disciplines like biology, chemistry, physics, economics, mathematics, psychology, philosophy. Each field has a few mental models that form the backbone of the topic. For example, some of the pillar mental models from economics include ideas like Incentives, Scarcity, and Economies of Scale.

If you can master the fundamentals of each discipline, then you can develop a remarkably accurate and useful picture of life. To quote Charlie Munger again, "80 or 90 important models will carry about 90 percent of the freight in making you a worldly-wise person. And, of those, only a mere handful really carry very heavy freight."

GENERAL THINKING CONCEPTS

Here are some concept of general thinking.

Occam's Razor

Simpler explanations are more likely to be true than complicated ones. This is the essence of Occam's Razor, a classic principle of logic and problem-solving. Instead of wasting your time trying to disprove complex scenarios, you can make decisions more confidently by basing them on the explanation that has the fewest moving parts.

First Principles Thinking

First principles thinking is one of the best ways to reverse-engineer complicated situations and unleash creative possibility. Sometimes called reasoning from first principles, it's a tool to help clarify complicated problems by separating the underlying ideas or facts from any assumptions based on them. What remains are the essentials. If you know the first principles of something, you can build the rest of your knowledge around them to produce something new.

The Map is not the Territory

The map of reality is not reality. Even the best maps are imperfect. That's because they are reductions of what they represent. If a map were to represent the territory with perfect fidelity, it would no longer be a reduction and thus would no longer be useful to us. A map can also be a snapshot of a point in time, representing something that no longer exists. This is important to keep in mind as we think through problems and make better decisions.

Inversion

Inversion is a powerful tool to improve your thinking because it helps you identify and remove obstacles to success. The root of inversion is "invert," which means to upend or turn upside down. As a thinking tool it means approaching a situation from the opposite end of the natural starting point. Most of us tend to think one way about a problem: forward. Inversion allows us to flip the problem around and think backward. Sometimes it's good to start at the beginning, but it can be more useful to start at the end.

Thought Experiment

Thought experiments can be defined as "devices of the imagination used to investigate the nature of things." Many disciplines, such as philosophy and physics, make use of thought experiments to examine what can be known. In doing so, they can open up new avenues for inquiry and exploration. Thought experiments are powerful because they help us learn from our mistakes and avoid future ones. They let us take on the impossible, evaluate the potential consequences of our actions, and re-examine history to make better decisions. They can help us both figure out what we really want, and the best way to get there.

Second-Order Thinking

Almost everyone can anticipate the immediate results of their actions. This type of first-order thinking is easy and safe but it's also a way to ensure you get the same results that everyone else gets. Second-order thinking is thinking farther ahead and thinking holistically. It requires us to not only consider our actions and their immediate consequences, but the subsequent effects of those actions as well.

Failing to consider the second and third order effects can unleash disaster.

Hanlon's Razor

Hard to trace in its origin, Hanlon's Razor states that we should not attribute to malice that which is more easily explained by stupidity. In a complex world, using this model helps us avoid paranoia and ideology. By not generally assuming that bad results are the fault of a bad actor, we look for options instead of missing opportunities. This model reminds us that people do make mistakes. It demands that we ask if there is another reasonable explanation for the events that have occurred. The explanation most likely to be right is the one that contains the least amount of intent.

Circle of Competence

When ego and not competence drives what we undertake, we have blind spots. If you know what you understand, you know where you have an edge over others. When you are honest about where your knowledge is lacking you know where you are vulnerable and where you can improve. Understanding your circle of competence improves decision making and outcomes.

Probabilistic Thinking

Probabilistic thinking is essentially trying to estimate, using some tools of math and logic, the likelihood of any specific outcome coming to pass. It is one of the best tools we have to improve the accuracy of our decisions. In a world where each moment is determined by an infinitely complex set of factors, probabilistic thinking helps us identify the most likely outcomes. When we know these our decisions can be more precise and effective.

This includes Fat-Tailed Processes

A process can often look like a normal distribution but have a large "tail" – meaning that seemingly outlier events are far more likely than they are in an actual normal distribution. A strategy or process may be far more risky than a normal distribution is capable of describing if the fat tail is on the negative side, or far more profitable if the fat tail is on the positive side. Much of the human social world is said to be fat-tailed rather than normally distributed.

The Bayesian method is a method of thought (named for Thomas Bayes) whereby one takes into account all prior relevant probabilities and then incrementally updates them as newer information arrives. This method is especially productive given the fundamentally non-deterministic world we experience: We must use prior odds and new information in combination to arrive at our best decisions. This is not necessarily our intuitive decision-making engine.

Systems

Network Effects

A network tends to become more valuable as nodes are added to the network: this is known as the network effect. An easy example is contrasting the development of the electricity system and the telephone system. If only one house has electricity, its inhabitants have gained immense value, but if only one house has a telephone, its inhabitants have gained nothing of use. Only with additional telephones does the phone network gain value. This network effect is widespread in the modern world and creates immense value for organizations and customers alike.

Via Negativa – Omission/Removal/Avoidance of Harm

In many systems, improvement is at best, or at times only, a result of removing bad elements rather than of adding good elements. This is a credo built into the modern medical profession: First, do no harm. Similarly, if one has a group of children behaving badly, removal of the instigator is often much more effective than any form of punishment meted out to the whole group.

Pareto Principle

Named for Italian polymath Vilfredo Pareto, who noticed that 80% of Italy's land was owned by about 20% of its population, the Pareto Principle states that a small amount of some phenomenon causes a disproportionately large effect. The Pareto Principle is an example of a power-law type of statistical distribution – as distinguished from a traditional bell curve – and is demonstrated in various phenomena ranging from wealth to city populations to important human habits.

Feedback Loops (and Homeostasis)

All complex systems are subject to positive and negative feedback loops whereby A causes B, which in turn influences A (and C), and so on – with higher-order effects frequently resulting from continual movement of the loop. In a homeostatic system, a change in A is often brought back into line by an opposite change in B to maintain the balance of the system, as with the temperature of the human body or the behavior of an organizational culture. Automatic feedback loops maintain a "static" environment unless and until an outside force changes the loop. A "runaway feedback loop" describes a situation in which the output of a reaction becomes its own catalyst (auto-catalysis).

The Lindy Effect

The Lindy Effect refers to the life expectancy of a non-perishable object or idea being related to its current lifespan. If an idea or object has lasted for X number of years, it would be expected (on average) to last another X years. Although a human being who is 90 and lives to 95 does not add 5 years to his or her life expectancy, non-perishables lengthen their life expectancy as they continually survive. A classic text is a prime example: if humanity has been reading Shakespeare's plays for 500 years, it will be expected to read them for another 500.

Scale

One of the most important principles of systems is that they are sensitive to scale. Properties (or behaviors) tend to change when you scale them up or down. In studying complex systems, we must always be roughly quantifying – in orders of magnitude, at least – the scale at which we are observing, analyzing, or predicting the system.

Emergence

Higher-level behavior tends to emerge from the interaction of lower-order components. The result is frequently not linear – not a matter of simple addition – but rather non-linear, or exponential. An important resulting property of emergent behavior is that it cannot be predicted from simply studying the component parts.

Irreducibility

We find that in most systems there are irreducible quantitative properties, such as complexity, minimums, time, and length. Below the irreducible level, the desired result simply does not occur. One cannot get several women pregnant to reduce the amount of time needed to have one child, and one cannot reduce a successfully built automobile to a single part. These results are, to a defined point, irreducible.

Tragedy of the Commons

A concept introduced by the economist and ecologist Garrett Hardin, the Tragedy of the Commons states that in a system where a common resource is shared, with no individual responsible for the wellbeing of the resource, it will tend to be depleted over time. The Tragedy is reducible to incentives: Unless people collaborate, each individual derives more personal benefit than the cost that he or she incurs, and therefore depletes the resource for fear of missing out.

Law of Diminishing Returns

Related to scale, most important real-world results are subject to an eventual decrease of incremental value. A good example would be a poor family: Give them enough money to thrive, and they are no longer poor. But after a certain point, additional money will not improve their lot; there is a clear diminishing return of additional dollars at some roughly quantifiable point. Often, the law of diminishing returns veers into negative territory – i.e., receiving too much money could destroy the poor family.

Chaos Dynamics (Butterfly Effect)/ (Sensitivity to Initial Conditions)

In a world such as ours, governed by chaos dynamics, small changes (perturbations) in initial conditions have massive downstream effects as near-infinite feedback loops occur; this phenomenon is also called the butterfly effect. This means that some aspects of physical systems (like the weather more than a few days from now) as well as social systems (the behavior of a group of human beings over a long period) are fundamentally unpredictable.

Preferential Attachment (Cumulative Advantage)

A preferential attachment situation occurs when the current leader is given more of the reward than the laggards, thereby tending to preserve or enhance the status of the leader. A strong network effect is a good example of preferential attachment; a market with 10x more buyers and sellers than the next largest market will tend to have a preferential attachment dynamic.

Gresham's Law

Gresham's Law, named for the financier Thomas Gresham, states that in a system of circulating currency, forged currency will tend to drive out real currency, as real currency is hoarded and forged currency is spent. We see a similar result in human systems, as with bad behavior driving out good behavior in a crumbling moral system, or bad practices driving out good practices in a crumbling economic system. Generally, regulation and oversight are required to prevent results that follow Gresham's Law.

Algorithms

While hard to precisely define, an algorithm is generally an automated set of rules or a "blueprint" leading a series of steps or actions resulting in a desired outcome, and often stated in the form of a series of "If → Then" statements. Algorithms are best known for their use in modern computing, but are a feature of biological life as well. For example, human DNA contains an algorithm for building a human being.

Margin of Safety

Similarly, engineers have also developed the habit of adding a margin for error into all calculations. In an unknown world, driving a 9,500-pound bus over a bridge built to hold precisely 9,600 pounds is rarely seen as intelligent. Thus, on the whole, few modern bridges ever fail. In practical life outside of physical engineering, we can often profitably give ourselves margins as robust as the bridge system.

Criticality

A system becomes critical when it is about to jump discretely from one phase to another. The marginal utility of the last unit before the phase change is wildly higher than any unit before it. A frequently cited example is water turning from a liquid to a vapor when heated to a specific temperature. "Critical mass" refers to the mass needed to have the critical event occur, most commonly in a nuclear system.

Renormalization Group

The renormalization group technique allows us to think about physical and social systems at different scales. An idea from physics, and a complicated one at that, the application of a renormalization group to social systems allows us to understand why a small number of stubborn individuals can have a disproportionate impact if those around them follow suit on increasingly large scales.

Fragility – Robustness – Antifragility

Popularized by Nassim Taleb, the sliding scale of fragility, robustness, and antifragility refers to the responsiveness of a system to incremental negative variability. A fragile system or object is one in which additional negative variability has a disproportionately negative impact, as with a coffee cup shattering from a 6-foot fall, but receiving no damage at all (rather than 1/6th of the damage) from a 1-foot fall. A robust system or object tends to be neutral to the additional negativity variability, and of course, an antifragile system benefits: If there were a cup that got stronger when dropped from 6 feet than when dropped from 1 foot, it would be termed antifragile.

Backup Systems/Redundancy

A critical model of the engineering profession is that of backup systems. A good engineer never assumes the perfect reliability of the components of the system. He or she builds in redundancy to protect the integrity of the total system. Without the application of this robustness principle, tangible and intangible systems tend to fail over time.

Spring-loading

A system is spring-loaded if it is coiled in a certain direction, positive or negative. Positively spring-loading systems and relationships is important in a fundamentally unpredictable world to help protect us against negative events. The reverse can be very destructive.

Complex Adaptive Systems

A complex adaptive system, as distinguished from a complex system in general, is one that can understand itself and change based on that understanding. Complex adaptive systems are social systems. The difference is best illustrated by thinking about weather prediction contrasted to stock market prediction. The weather will not change based on an important forecaster's opinion, but the stock market might. Complex adaptive systems are thus fundamentally not predictable.

Physical World

Alloying

When we combine various elements, we create new substances. This is no great surprise, but what can be surprising in the alloying process is that 2+2 can equal not 4 but 6 – the alloy can be far stronger than the simple addition of the underlying elements would lead us to believe. This process leads us to engineer great physical objects, but we understand many intangibles in the same way; a combination of the right elements in social systems or even individuals can create a 2+2=6 effect similar to alloying.

Viscosity

Viscosity is the "measure of how hard it is for one layer of fluid to slide over another layer." If a liquid is hard to move it is more viscous. If it is more viscous there is more resistance. Viscosity isn't usually an issue for humans. We have to deal with gravity and inertia, although viscosity is always present. But for small particles, gravity and inertia become a non-issue compared to viscosity. We thus learn that when we change the scale we change what forces are relevant.

Laws of Thermodynamics

The laws of thermodynamics describe energy in a closed system. The laws cannot be escaped and underlie the physical world. They describe a world in which useful energy is constantly being lost, and energy cannot be created or destroyed. Applying their lessons to the social world can be a profitable enterprise.

Relativity

Relativity has been used in several contexts in the world of physics, but the important aspect to study is the idea that an observer cannot truly understand a system of which he himself is a part. For example, a man inside an airplane does not feel like he is experiencing movement, but an outside observer can see that movement is occurring. This form of relativity tends to affect social systems in a similar way.

Activation Energy

A fire is not much more than a combination of carbon and oxygen, but the forests and coal mines of the world are not combusting at will because such a chemical reaction requires the input of a critical level of "activation energy" in order to get a reaction started. Two combustible elements alone are not enough.

Catalysts

A catalyst either kick-starts or maintains a chemical reaction, but isn't itself a reactant. The reaction may slow or stop without the addition of catalysts. Social systems, of course, take on many similar traits, and we can view catalysts in a similar light.

Reciprocity

If I push on a wall, physics tells me that the wall pushes back with equivalent force. In a biological system, if one individual acts on another, the action will tend to be reciprocated in kind. And of course, human beings act with intense reciprocity demonstrated as well.

Velocity

Velocity is not equivalent to speed; the two are sometimes confused. Velocity is speed plus vector: how fast something gets somewhere. An object that moves two steps forward and then two steps back has moved at a certain speed but shows no velocity. The addition of the vector, that critical distinction, is what we should consider in practical life.

Leverage

Most of the engineering marvels of the world have been accomplished with applied leverage. As famously stated by Archimedes, "Give me a lever long enough and I shall move the world." With a small amount of input force, we can make a great output force through leverage. Understanding where we can apply this model to the human world can be a source of great success.

Inertia

An object in motion with a certain vector wants to continue moving in that direction unless acted upon. This is a fundamental physical principle of motion; however, individuals, systems, and organizations display the same effect. It allows them to minimize the use of energy, but can cause them to be destroyed or eroded.

MENTAL MODELS - THE SECOND DISCIPLINE OF LEARNING ORGANIZATIONS

"My boss never listens to anything I have to say. He'll ask for my opinion then do just what he was planning to in the first place. Why bother?"

"My employees don't really care much about their work. The only thing that seems to motivate them is the end of the week. Guess I'll just have to do it myself."

Sound familiar? Those are two different views of the same situation. They are mental models in action, and they reinforce a negative pattern of behavior that is ultimately destructive to an organization in many ways.

What skills do individuals need to develop?

So how does one break out of this type of downward spiral? The first step is to recognize the gap between what we believe to be true and what is actually true, or to put it more precisely, the gap between mental models and current reality. There are two main areas of skills in which individuals can practice working with mental models:

- Skills of reflection and
- Skills of inquiry.

Skills of reflection involve slowing down our thinking so that we become more aware of how we form our mental models and how they influence our behavior. We can do this in several ways. One way is to become more aware of recognizing when we make what are often referred to as "leaps of abstraction," that is making generalizations based on our observations with no data to back it up. In the manager-employee example, the employee observes the manager asking for an opinion but then not acting upon it. The employee then jumps to the conclusion that the manger really isn't interested in subordinates' ideas. In turn, the manager observes disengagement and concludes that it must be because the employees don't really care about their work. One way to avoid this pitfall is to ask the questions:

- "What is the data on which my beliefs or generalizations are based?"
- "Have I ever seen any disconfirming evidence to my beliefs?"
- "Am I willing to consider the possibility that my beliefs may be inaccurate?"

Another method for developing skills of reflection is often referred to as exposing the "left-hand column." The "left-hand column" represents thoughts we often have during conversations but do not articulate. By actually writing these thoughts down after the fact, we are making our mental models visible. For example, the manager who views his employees as disinterested may call a meeting of his department to announce a new strategic direction for his team. After presenting the idea, he asks for reaction and is met with stony silence. His immediate thought may be, "Man! What is it going to take to light a fire under these people?" If an employee responds with tepid support, he might also think, "Oh geez! Here we go with the lip service again! Can't they think for themselves?" Each of these responses reinforces the manager's mental model, but writing them down makes it possible for him to distance himself enough from the belief to begin to recognize it for what it is, a generalization.

A final technique for developing skills of reflection is to recognize the gap between what we say we believe, our espoused theory, and what we actually do, our theory in use. Put another way, we must start comparing our words to our actions or behaviors. Using the manager-employee example again, the manager may truly believe that participative decision-making creates a productive team, but his behavior is not sending that message to his employees. Until he recognizes that gap, no learning or change can occur.

Skills of inquiry shape how we operate in face-to-face interactions. Once we have begun to practice our skills of reflection, we can then begin to surface and discuss our mental models with others. In doing so, we must remember that our mental models are only pieces to the puzzle. In The Skilled Facilitator, Roger Schwarz has developed a technique called the mutual learning model that can help individuals hone their interpersonal skills. It is based on the assumptions that everyone sees things differently, and it is those differences that create opportunities for learning and creativity. It is also based on the belief that everyone is acting with integrity. One can practice the mutual learning model by:

- Testing your assumptions by articulating them and asking for confirming or disconfirming evidence;
- Sharing all relevant information: withholding information will only lead to a less complete picture;
- Being transparent by putting your thinking on the table rather than your finished thought;

- Focusing on interests, not positions, that is, talking about and agreeing to outcomes before jumping to solutions;
- Discussing those thoughts in the "left-hand column" that are often driving your actions;
- Balancing advocacy with inquiry, that is, asking about other points of view as much as you explain your own.

These skills, in combination with the skills of reflection, will unleash the power to change mental models and to begin moving the organization toward sustainable change. In order to change our behavior we must first change the beliefs upon which those behaviors are based.

How can organizations transform mental models from barrier to leverage point?

Working with mental models is the most difficult place to start building a learning organization but can yield the greatest amount of change. Developing and shaping mental models means changing both individual and organizational behavior - a tall order at best. It is a process that requires patience and perseverance. The following conditions will help organizations reduce the barriers to surfacing and examining mental models:

Create a safe environment in which employees feel comfortable surfacing and examining their mental models; it must also be an environment where decisions are based on what's best for the organization, not on politics;

- Help your employees develop their skills of reflection and inquiry;

- Promote diversity rather than conformity;
- Agree to disagree; everyone does not need to agree with the various mental models that exist; each one is just an additional piece of information;
- Be comfortable with uncertainty; we will never know the complete story.

This process requires individuals and organizations alike to change how they think about the nature of work. Once those barriers are reduced, an organization can begin to see mental models become leverage points for innovation. Those negative reinforcing loops transform into upward spirals of success.

How to Spot a Common Mental Error That Leads to Misguided Thinking

Human beings have been blaming strange behavior on the full moon for centuries. In the Middle Ages, for example, people claimed that a full moon could turn humans into werewolves. In the 1700s, it was common to believe that a full moon could cause epilepsy or feverish temperatures. We even changed our language to match our beliefs. The word lunatic comes from the Latin root luna, which means moon.

Today, we have (mostly) come to our senses. While we no longer blame sickness and disease on the phases of the moon, you will hear people use it as a casual explanation for crazy behavior. For example, a common story in medical circles is that during a chaotic evening at the hospital one of the nurses will often say, "Must be a full moon tonight."

There is little evidence that a full moon actually impacts our behaviors. A complete analysis of more than 30 peer-reviewed studies found no correlation between a full moon and hospital admissions, casino payouts, suicides, traffic accidents, crime rates, and many other common events.

How We Fool Ourselves Without Realizing It

An illusory correlation happens when we mistakenly over-emphasize one outcome and ignore the others. For example, let's say you visit New York City and someone cuts you off as you're boarding the subway train. Then, you go to a restaurant and the waiter is rude to you. Finally, you ask someone on the street for directions and they blow you off. When you think back on your trip to New York it is easy to remember these experiences and conclude that "people from New York are rude" or "people in big cities are rude."

However, you are forgetting about all of the meals you ate when the waiter acted perfectly normal or the hundreds of people you passed on the Subway platform who didn't cut you off. These were literally non-events because nothing notable happened. As a result, it is easier to remember the times someone acted rudely toward you than the times when you dined happily or took the subway in peace.

Here's where the brain science comes into play:

Hundreds of psychology studies have proven that we tend to overestimate the importance of events we can easily recall and underestimate the importance of events we have trouble recalling. The easier it is to remember, the more likely we are to create a strong relationship between two things that are weakly related or not related at all.

BEING OPEN-MINDED

Being open-minded can be really tough sometimes. Most of us are brought up with a set of beliefs and values and, throughout our lives, tend to surround ourselves with people who share the same values and beliefs. Therefore, it can be difficult when we're faced with ideas that challenge our own and, though we may wish to be open-minded, we may struggle with the act of it from time to time.

I'd like to say I'm a fairly open-minded person, but, like most people, I do have some pretty strong views about specific topics and find it hard to sway from those opinions -- no matter how others might try to persuade me. Of course, I fully believe that having strong beliefs can be a wonderful thing and I believe we should all stay true to what we believe in, but having strong beliefs doesn't have to mean having a closed mind.

Though it can be tough to do sometimes, I've always found that when I open my mind, I've reaped a lot of rewarding benefits. There is much to be gained from opening the door to your mind and letting new ideas and beliefs come in. Here are just a few of the benefits I've uncovered when I've taken the time to view the world around me with an open mind...

Benefits of Being Open-Minded

Check out these benefits of being open minded.

Strengthening yourself.

Open-mindedness provides a platform on which you can build, piling one idea on top of another. With an open mind, you can learn about new things and you can use the new ideas to build on the old ideas. Everything you experience can add up, strengthening who you are and what you believe in. It's very hard to build on experiences without an open mind.

Letting go of control.

When you open your mind, you free yourself from having to be in complete control of your thoughts. You allow yourself to experience new ideas and thoughts and you challenge the beliefs you currently have. It can be very liberating to look at the world through an open mind.

Experiencing changes.

Opening up your mind to new ideas allows you to the opportunity to change what you think and how you view the world. Now, this doesn't mean you necessarily will change your beliefs, but you have the option to when you think with an open mind.

Making mistakes.

Making mistakes doesn't seem like it would be much of a benefit, but it truly is. When you open your mind and allow yourself to see things from others' perspectives, you allow yourself not only to recognize potential mistakes you've made, but also to make new mistakes. Doesn't sound like much fun, but it's a great thing to fall and get back up again.

Gaining confidence.

When you live with an open mind, you have a strong sense of self. You are not confined by your own beliefs, nor are you confined by the beliefs of others. For that reason, you are able to have and gain confidence as you learn more and more about the world around you. Open-mindedness helps you to learn and grow, strengthening your belief in yourself.

Making yourself vulnerable.

One of the scariest (and greatest) things about seeing the world through an open mind is making yourself vulnerable. In agreeing to have an open-minded view of the world, you're admitting you don't know everything and that there are possibilities you may not have considered. This vulnerability can be both terrifying and exhilarating.

Being honest.

There is an honesty that comes with an open mind because being open-minded means admitting that you aren't all-knowing. It means believing that whatever truth you find might always have more to it than you realize. This understanding creates an underlying sense of honesty that permeates the character of anyone who lives with an open mind.

For some, being open-minded is easy; it comes as effortlessly as breathing. For others, having an open mind can be more of a challenge, something that they have to work on and make an effort to obtain. Whether or not you consider yourself to be open-minded, you can certainly see from the list above that there are great benefits to viewing life with an open mind. It's not always an easy thing to do (believe me, most people struggle with this), but the effort to think openly and embrace new ideas will be worth it when you're able to take part in the benefits that come from opening your mind.

Reasons to Always Keep an Open Mind

Maintaining an open mind in your daily interactions with people is extremely necessary if you really want to keep moving forward, be it in your career, your small business, your educational pursuits or your relationship.

Let's take a look at the reasons why you need to keep an open mind.

You will nurture stronger relationships.

It doesn't mean that you should trust all manner of people just because you desire to build relationships either for your small business or for career development.

The actual point here is that you cannot expect to have strong, meaningful relationships with others if you're not willing to allow yourself time to find out more about their values and hidden attributes.

In other words, there is no way we will be able to build closer ties with our partners or develop beneficial networks with our suppliers or agents if all we do is prejudge their actions or motives.

And remember, the more relationships you're able to build by being positive and open-minded, the more you will be contributing to making our world a better place.

Reality could be different from appearances.

For all you know, that individual seeking employment at your startup and whom you consider to have nothing to offer, just because of something you don't like about their appearance could turn out to be the single most valuable employee you will ever have.

It isn't always that people put their best foot forward whenever they have to meet new situations. Some of us simply don't know how to apply the principle of making a good initial impression. That is the reason why you have to keep an open mind when dealing with people you've never met before. It is highly likely that you'll be in for a pleasant surprise if you give others the chance to prove their worth over a reasonable period of time.

Trust me, companies embarking on a talent-hunt, people looking for relationship partners, students in search for a good school or adult learning center to acquire more life skills are known to have lost what could have been their best choices ever, just by dismissing prospects based on appearances.

You cannot afford to make that costly mistake.

You will learn valuable lessons and grow further if you always keep an open mind.

No one has ever known it all. That is why we always have to keep on finding ways and opportunities to learn and know more. Sometimes, we learn our most valuable lessons from the most unlikely places, experiences and people. Knowledge is always evolving. What is believed to be the best method of solving a problem becomes obsolete within a short period of time. The knowledge you acquired from school years ago may not be that relevant the way it was at the time you graduated.

To remain relevant, therefore, you and I need to keep an open mind and stop being negative about the new developments going on all around us. The more we're prepared to try new ideas, immerse ourselves wholeheartedly in new experiences and even learn from people who may be many years our juniors, the greater the skills we'll acquire to enable us to continue to achieve more.

Maintaining an open mind opens doors.

How many times have you been surprised with an opportunity from someone or from an activity you least expect to deliver? Quite a lot, I presume.

We live in a world full of surprises. That door you never thought could lead to your success could be the one bringing great wealth to those who believed.That is a good reason for you to maintain a positive attitude and keep your mind open always.

The truth is, there are many employers out there who still value open-minded and adventurous employees. At a highly competitive job or promotion interview, for example, chances are that those who display a strong willingness to keep an open mind to continue learning are the ones likely to be shortlisted for consideration.

On the other hand, those who display an attitude of being very conservative and rigid with their opinions or traditional thinking would hardly stand any chance.

Ways to Become an Open Minded Person

Here are some ways to become an open minded, Even if You See Yourself as Hopelessly Dull

When You Find Yourself Making Assumptions – Stop

Making too many assumptions is an open mindedness killer. If you find yourself continually saying the following things:

- I would never like that.
- I just don't relate to people who…
- That's just not my thing.
- I would never fit in with…
- I don't think I would be welcome…
- People who live like that are all…

First, become aware of the fact that you do it. Then, make a dedicated effort to stop yourself and then rephrase your assumption. Instead of assuming that you would never like something, restate your thought to say, you aren't sure if you would like something but are willing to give it a try.

Set a Goal to Experience at Least One New Thing Each Month

To a large extent, becoming more open minded is an action oriented endeavor. To get the results that you want, you have to take action and do things to widen your horizons. Your first step can be selecting one new thing to experience each month. Your possibilities are nearly limitless. If you aren't sure where to begin, here are a few suggestions:

- Read a book or magazine that isn't from your preferred genre
- Try a new cuisine
- Write a letter to the editor
- Visit a new neighborhood
- Spend a day volunteering with a population you are not familiar with
- Spend a day with your radio tuned to a new station

Widen Your Circle of Friends

This one is easier said than done, but it is so important. The wider your circle of friends, the more likely you will be exposed to different ideas and belief systems. This is key to becoming a more open minded person. Obviously, you cannot force a friendship to happen, but you can take steps to make it more likely. For example, you can join a club, or start up a new hobby. Even something as simple as speaking to a different co-worker during your lunch break can make a difference.

Examine Your Hot Button Issues From Another Perspective

Remember that opening your mind doesn't mean changing it. It means learning to view the world from more than one point of view, and to consider multiple possibilities. Take some time to think about a few of your hot button issues. These are issues that you feel very strongly about. They might be related to politics, religion, parenting, or morals. Close minded people tend to see these issues in very binary terms. People are either right or wrong in their views, and the people who are wrong are either morally or intellectually inferior to those who are right. Unfortunately, this attitude does very little for fostering understanding. It also does little to broaden your horizons. However, if you make an effort to understand why somebody has a different view of an issue, you will often find that their views aren't due to moral shortcomings or other character flaws. Instead, they are just a product of that person's life experience.

Learn to go With The Flow

Mental and emotional rigidity are two things that are sure to get in your way as you try to become more open minded. If you constantly tell yourself you shouldn't try new things, or convince yourself that the consequences will be dire, you will continue to be closed minded. Try to relax more often and just let life happen. Chances are, you will find that breaking or at least relaxing some of the rules and restrictions you place on your life actually leads to good things. You'll be much happier if you adopt a live and let live attitude, not just with others, but also with yourself.

Learn to Question Yourself

The next time you find yourself saying no to a new experience, or convincing yourself that there is no way you could ever, enjoy, believe, or understand something, take a moment to ask yourself why? What is holding you back? Is it fear or prejudice? The more you explore the reasons you tend to close yourself off, the better able you will be to resist those impulses and open your mind.

Let Yourself be Vulnerable

There's no way to be more open minded in your thought processes or your actions without letting yourself be vulnerable. If you try new things, reach out to new people, and attempt to embrace new ideas, you will, on occasion, fail or be disappointed. If you accept that and allow yourself to be vulnerable, you will soon find that even when things don't go as planned, things are still okay. Even better, you can still get something positive out of a negative experience. Remember that the failure you may experience can also be used as a launching pad for reaching your goals.

The Pros And Cons Of An Open Mind

An open mind is good thing - most of the time. New ideas, new experience, increased knowledge, personal and professional growth, better relationships and an overall positive approach to life are just a few of the benefits of having an open mind. However, there are some pitfalls. Like an open window or an open door in which bugs can enter the home, an open mind is susceptible to litter, junk, lies and deceptions, false information and misdirection. The open mind, like an open window, needs a screen to keep the bugs out. The mental screen is called "discrimination." It is an attribute everyone has. Discrimination is the capacity to see differences. Like any tool, discrimination can be used wisely or foolishly, for good or for bad. Unless we want our open mind filled with all kinds of non-sense, we must learn to differentiate between what is of genuine value and what is junk. You might say that our discriminative capacity is like an email spam filter. We can set the parameters to filter out the junk and let in the useful information. Generally, what is important to us is considered useful and gets through. What is important to you? An open mind, with a screen to prevent the bugs from entering, or a spam filter to block the junk, is a wonderful thing.

The open mind is also susceptible to a lack of conviction. Too many conflicting ideas can enter an open mind and cause indecision. It is necessary now and then to close the mind, disallow any more input, make a decision and act. Perhaps more important than having an open mind is having a mind that is capable of being open - or closed. We need a mind with hinges - well lubricated and in good working order. The hinges of our mind is our ability to decide. We can decide to accept or reject information. We can decide to consider a point of view or not. We can decide to open or close the window. A home would become cold and drafty if the doors and windows could not be closed now and then. But, it would be awfully stuffy if they could not be opened. We simply decide to open or close the window - or the mind. But, our decision must be made from intelligence and reason, not emotional reactions. Anemotionally reactive person would likely open the doors and windows during a blizzard - or close the mind to beneficial information.It's the mind that remains closed that prevents creative growth.

It's the closed mind that stated in the late 1870's that the telephone had too many shortcomings to be seriously considered as a communication device or in the early 1970's that no one would ever want a computer in their home. Charles Duell, the Commissioner of the U.S. Office of Patents in 1899 said "Everything that can be invented has been invented." In 1981, Bill Gates, founder of Microsoft, said "640K ought to be enough for anybody." Even the most visionary person may close their mind to possibilities. Perhaps there is a bit more effort in keeping the mind open, just as smiling requires a little more muscle movement. But, the results of a smile are so often rewarding - and the fruits of an open mind can be very enriching. Despite the predictions of "experts" quoted above, it appears the mind will strive to be open and will move forward into new experiences hitherto thought unavailable or unreachable.

Ultimately, the cons of an open mind can be dealt with and the pros of an open mind are too important to neglect. As Charles Kettering, the American engineer and inventor said, "Where there is an open mind, there will be a frontier." Living as we do on the verge of global catastrophes, we need a frontier. We need a vision of a better future, and a path towards that future. For that, we will need an open mind.

Maximize Your Potential by Being Open Minded

If you want to maximize your potential for success in business and in life, you've got to be open minded. Don't limit yourself - there are so many great things that you can do and accomplish if you open yourself to the world and open your eyes to the things that are available for you.

Perhaps you've become accustomed to some routines and patterns. You only see things in black and white because you've gotten used to this kind of thinking - just more of the same. However, despite what you perceive as commonplace in your everyday life and environment, if you're open minded, you'll definitely see more and allow more. Don't limit yourself to a small box and the small and ordinary ways of thinking.

Maximize your potential because you deserve more!

By limiting yourself, you're assuming that nothing else is going to happen, nothing is going to change, and that you're powerless. Do you ever think that way?

If you remain open minded to all of the possibilities in life, you'll see that life is so much more than some small place - opportunities are abundant. So if you wish to maximize your potential and truly make the most out of the opportunities that come your way, you should learn how to think out of the box by following these tips:

- Rely on and trust yourself when making decisions. If you've become accustomed to relying on people for your actions, stop this practice. Instead, start making decisions for yourself. If you used to look up to someone for the things that you have to do, this is the time for you to take charge and take the lead to maximize your potential. It's now time for you to go out of your comfort zone and get out of your box.

- Question things. Who said that you must accept things as they are? If something confuses you or you don't understand what's going on, don't hesitate to question it. If your ignorance and innocence is limiting your reach, it's especially important to remember to be open minded - spread your arms and your mind to widen your reach.

- Learn to think beyond what is in front of you. When you deal with things, always view it not just in relation to what you have at the moment, but also to what it could bring for your future that could potentially help you maximize your potential. You need to understand that everything is connected, and your power to anticipate and think ahead, can and will make wonders for you.

Maximize your potential because you can!

- Feel free to make mistakes. It's nice to take risks from time to time. If you're too frightened to move out of your box because you're afraid of making mistakes, you will never get to see what's outside. You may trip and you may fall. Don't worry about making a mistake. Instead, think of what you'll do when you get where you want to go.

- Let other people inspire you. If you cannot see yourself going out of the box, then try to visualize yourself through other people's lives. Study other people's achievements and marvel at what they have accomplished. Let their achievements inspire you to achieve more for yourself. Believe that if they were able to do it, you can do it for yourself as well.

- Continue learning. Explore other things that you've not tried before. Go places, try new adventures, learn and feed on your zest for knowledge because these things will broaden your horizon and allow you to go beyond what most people expect of you.

Open minded people have the greatest power to maximize their potential. It's all about thinking differently - getting out of the box that limits you. It's completely up to you. As you encounter people and discover programs that promise to help you maximize your potential, keep in mind that it's your responsibility to take action. Take what you're learning and make it your own. Your ultimate success depends on it!

POWER OF THE MIND

One thing that you need to know is that the power of the mind is something that we need to have in the palm of our hands. For one thing, the human race is one that has not been realising the full power of the noggin. According to science and the halls of medicine, we are not using the full potential of the mind, and in this case, it means that more than 70% of the brain that is residing within our skulls is not being used to its full potential and this is the really tragic part of everything. We need to know that there is more that we can do and the first thing that we must look at is really what we are doing that makes our brain so inert and inactive in the first place.

This means that we have been underutilised, we have been walking around the world today with only 20% of our brain in use, and it boggles the mind to how much potential we are actually wasting. At the end of the day, what we need to do is to not underestimate the power of the mind, and how we can do this is look at the technology that has been around for a long time now, and from there postulate the actual potential power the mind has.

We are capable of some wonderful things, and this is even more possible by the fact that we are then able to manipulate the world around us and respond when we are under duress. One thing that we need to know is that the world that exists around us is one that is constantly bombarding us with ideas that we should not be taking if we want our minds to perform at its maximum capacity. In all sense of the word, we are living in convenience, which means that we have to think less to survive, and for all intents and purposes when it comes to evolution, this means that we have placed a great anchor on our journey towards evolution.

How can we evolve anymore in any sense, if we have no need to utilise any more of our brain, and because according to many geneticists all over the world, the last key of evolution is in our minds, and once we have crossed that final human frontier, then are we able to move on from there and look at the world around us with a different perspective. One of the things that we need to know is how we are going to unlock the power of the mind, and there is different technology out there that can be achieved with something as simple as this. For one thing, you can look at things like subliminal audio and the ever popular binaural beats technology, which uses simple sound waves to effect a response in the cortical of the brain and make it a much better performer under different conditions - augmenting the power of the mind.

In our quest for success, more creativity, goal achievement, and a multitude of other embodiments of personal growth...there are special components of the mind that can be utilized to accelerate our growth exponentially. When we talk about the mind, it's important to realize that our total mind is actually made up of three separate components...that when used properly together, can virtually guarantee success in almost any endeavor.

The conscious, subconscious, and superconscious minds are the powerful parts that make up the total mind...and the best part is that we all possess these wonderful tools of the mind! Each of these aspects of the mind are vital pieces that were designed by our Creator to help us achieve all of our dreams, goals, and desires.

Now that we know what they are...lets define each aspect of the mind a little. Then we can discuss how these powerful components of the total mind can be utilized together in the way they were always intended to be.

Conscious Mind: The Programmer

The first mind component we will talk about is probably the one we are all most familiar with. The conscious mind is what many call the reasoning mind or decision making mind. When many of us are talking about the mind, the conscious mind is what we are actually referring to.

It is through the conscious mind that we make all our decisions from...and form all of our beliefs from. We use the conscious mind to reason through the data presented to us...and then assign priorities and tasks based on our current belief systems.

Along with those aspects of the conscious mind just discussed, another very important function of the conscious mind...is to set goals that can basically be programmed into the subconscious mind. This programming aspect of the conscious mind is a very powerful tool for the achievement of goals...because it sets in motion the incredible computing and problem solving functions of the subconscious mind.

Subconscious Mind: The Biological Machine

As the title of this section suggest...the subconscious mind can be thought of as a biological computing machine with immense powers for problem solving. The subconscious mind is truly the workhorse for our entire mind.

The subconscious mind is the portion of the mind that controls all of our automatic bodily functions such as controlling vital organs associated with blood flow, digestion, etc. The subconscious mind is also the mind component that controls the release of vital hormones that can stimulate such things as the "fight or flight" response when we feel threatened by external forces.

The subconscious mind is also the seat for all of our stored memories. Just like a computer...the subconscious mind can utilize the vast amount of stored memories to help solve problems and come up with creative solutions. Therefore, it is important for us to try and gain as much knowledge about as many subjects as possible...because the subconscious mind may be able to use external data and the stored information we have in our memories to formulate new solutions to problems, and plans towards any goals we may have.

In regards to the successful achievement of our goals...it is very important that we try to form new positive habits. In essence, the subconscious mind has the ability to take regular thought patterns and actions...and turn them into positive habits that can really accelerate our personal growth and ability to achieve our dreams and desires. Another great reason for developing positive habits is that we can also induce our superconscious mind to come into play...and that's when some really "miraculous" things can start to occur in our lives.

Superconscious Mind: The Universal Mind

When we utilize the superconscious mind, we are going beyond our physical bodies...and into the spiritual realms. The superconscious mind is in fact referred by many as the human spirit, soul, or universal mind. As an actual fragment of God itself, our souls have incredible powers and connections that go way beyond our physical reality.

Because of the Universal Mind's unique connection to all other minds and Infinite Intelligence...many psychic powers are possible as we engage our superconsciousness. Extrasensory Perception (ESP), Telepathy, Telekinesis, and Clairvoyance are just some of the amazing psychic abilities available to those who learn how to truly tap into the powers of the Superconscious Mind.

Along with the amazing psychic abilities available to each of us, being tapped into the Universal Mind allows us the opportunity to access the vast amount of knowledge that is part of the Superconscious Mind. Throughout history there has been many names given for this vast storehouse of knowledge...and incredibly, this powerful information base is available for anyone who learns how to tap into it.

In regards to the successful achievement of our goals and desires...the superconscious mind can be engaged to bring into our lives certain opportunities and synchronicities that can help accelerate the accomplishment of our life goals and dreams. In conjunction with our subconscious minds and the positive habits it helps create...our superconscious minds can work in the spiritual realms to help bring our hopes and dreams into reality.

Using the powerful components of the total mind to virtually achieve anything we set our minds to

By now I'm hoping you are beginning to realize the incredible tools of the mind you possess...and even more amazing, is the fact that each and every one of us has these same powerful mind tools at our disposal.

To help ingrain the functions of each mind component...lets go through a quick set of steps we might use to achieve a specific goal.

First, because of how vital it is to insure we are programming the right goal for ourselves...we should spend some time contemplating our specific goal to make sure it is the correct one for ourselves. Once we have truly determined what we wish to accomplish...we then need to "program" it into our subconscious mind through the use of meditation, visualization, affirmations, self talk, etc.

With a firm goal input to our subconscious mind...we then step back and let the subconscious mind utilize our stored memories and all the data that our senses bring in...to begin coming up with the best plans of action for achieving our goal. As the subconscious mind prompts us towards action steps...we must then start performing the necessary actions given to us...while always remembering that these action steps should come naturally to us.

Sometimes our goals are so big (and there is nothing wrong with that)... that they require the help of the superconscious mind. As prompted by the subconscious mind, the superconscious mind will begin to tap into the vast storehouse of knowledge and spiritual connections it has available to itself...to bring into our lives the opportunities and synchronicities that can truly bring your hopes and dreams into reality.

How to Stick to Your Personal Goals

Setting a goal is a very significant thing in your personal life and business as well. A whole lot of self-help literature on the subject emphasize the need for setting goals for ourselves. Personal goal setting is a process that needs some stages to work through in order for you to achieve successful goals. Normal goals are required to be specific and measurable. Once you set a precise goal and put in dates and amount of time needed so that you can measure the achievement then you are good to go. Ask yourself the question: "what exactly will I be doing after I achieve this goal?". Personal goals allow you to determine your direction and help you to strive towards reaching the destination. As we are going to see,goal setting is essential and has many benefits.

If you have no goals or plans, then opportunities will often mean nothing to you. Opportunities become opportunities only when you recognize them as ideas you can implement to assist you toward your goal. Spending your energy having goals and achieving them is every bit worthwhile, except when you act out of your ego. When people do something out of their personal egos they tend to resist,over and over and spend much more energy to realize their goals in the process.

- The first thing for you to do is to define your goals and to make sure that you judge them all the time. Define the purpose of your goal with passion and conviction. A 3-by-5 inch card with the target goal printed on top is real handy. Using the same passion and conviction you first wrote it, read it aloud on a daily basis.
- Practice focusing on one goal for at least a month and then turn it into a habit. For example, if you want to run a marathon you want to create the habit of running every day. The rule of thumb here is to focus on things you can control. Also, make it your responsibility to follow through on your goals.
- It is the creative powers of the mind that form the key to happiness and that can bring to your life anything you ever wanted. If you learn how to set goals, develop action plans and

pull together a like-minded team of individuals,whatever it is that you desire will eventually manifest itself. This as such is the power of the subconscious mind. It only awaits the stimulation of your desire to spring forth and bring your desires to reality. You possess the key to the door and that key,ultimately, is your subconscious mind. It is in our mind that thoughts -- imagination, reasoning and intellect--including our emotions and willpower are created. And in here lies the very heart of the individual--the subconscious.

The Power of the Mind & Mental Models: Our Potential for Life

You may have heard the phrase, "What you see is what you get." It implies that our view of the world inhibits our ability to experience it. Few would argue with the fact that a person who has never experienced love in their lives has a great deal of difficulty finding, maintaining, or sustaining a first-class relationship. In a similar fashion if you've grown up in abject poverty, it takes a great deal of personal transformation before you can live with abundance easily. This book explores the similarities between the mystic tradition of "the power of the mind " and the scientific or organizational development tradition of "mental models." We all want something. Playing with these ideas leads us down the road where we are more likely to get it.

As a long-held mystic tradition, alchemy, which you may have heard of to mean the ability to change lead into gold, deals with the ability to change an experience which is heavy laden to one that is full of potential and abundance through the transformation of our ideas. Changing the bad to the good using the power of our minds has been a topic that surfaces periodically through human history. The most recent and widespread form has been the movie The Secret and the proliferation of some very good teachers, such as Jerry and Esther Hicks. People who work with the power of the mind build upon the idea that the 'subconscious' might also allow us to be in touch with the life force of the universe. Through meditation, and other processes that open our consciousness to more than what we are aware of in our limited form, we will have access to ideas that take our lives in new and unexpected directions. Jerry and Esther Hicks add the emotion to this mix and teach us that our 'emotional guidance system' always lets us know if we are on track with ourselves by whether or not we experience happiness and lightness in our lives.

Mental models can be traced back to the work of Kenneth Craik in 1943 when he suggested that the human mind constructs small-scale models of reality that it uses to anticipate events. He went on to suggest that mental model can be constructed from perception, our imagination, or the norms of the lives we lead in the times we live. The interesting point here is that mental models tie closely to visual images and can be abstract. Have you ever looked at a drawing of someone's idea, and "gotten it"instantly? That is the power of the mental model. Jay Wright Forrester defined them as:

"The image of the world around us, which we carry in our head, is just a model. Nobody in his head imagines all the world, government or country. He has only selected concepts, and relationships between them, and uses those to represent the real system."

While Senge explains:

"Mental models are deeply ingrained assumptions, generalizations, or even pictures or images that influence how we understand the world and how we take action"

What is common to both of these is the idea that, until we realize the limits of our thinking, or mental models we can't change them. Once aware, our ability to take action on new ideas is greatly enhanced.

How to Begin Mastering The Power of the Mind

Are you familiar with the power of the mind? You have certainly heard of the concept of "mind over matter," but do you really comprehend its true potential power in your everyday life? Hypnotists have used this concept to an extreme to cause people to believe the thoughts that are fed into their subconscious mind instead of their actual current physical situation.

Some people who have intense irrational fear learn to dispel these fears by developing their ability to create a safe environment in their mind based on the power of suggestion. If you are for example afraid of heights, perhaps you have convinced yourself that it isn't so high, that you cannot fall and that you are really safe and in no danger. Such simple suggestions of thoughts and beliefs can keep people thinking rationally in all kinds of situations.

The opposite is certainly possible as well. People who are afraid of the dark can easily freak themselves out by imagining that something is there waiting to get or worse harm them. By thinking with a logical thought process, a person knows there is nothing in the dark and can tell themselves this, by creating a safe visualization that will result in a calming feeling.

These are childish examples, but the success of competent people can be hindered by negative thoughts of "monsters in the dark" and "falling from high places." Positive thinking should replace negative ideas if you want to appreciate the true power of your mind.

The subconscious mind power is very powerful in transforming mental information into reality. In order to appreciate lasting happiness with the power of suggestion, you must develop a habit of regularly meditating. Consider it a mild hypnosis where you focus on relaxing your brain so your daily consciousness will recall the emotion experienced during meditation.

Believe in your efforts to meditate as you attempt to achieve your full potential. This is a natural requirement to benefiting from positive affirmations. You cannot expect meditating to do you any good if your subconscious mind keeps repeating that it is a waste of time?

A great time to meditate as you begin learning more about the power of thought in your daily life is just before you fall asleep. Think about tomorrow and what creative thing you will do to further your attempts at mastering the power of your subconscious mind. Sleep is a time for you to receive inspiration from your subconscious, so keep a notebook by your bed, and be prepared to write down what comes to mind when you first awaken.

Using the Power of the Mind to Attract Success

Some people may not know this, but the mind is a very powerful tool, that if used effectively, you can attract wealth, success and love. The power of the mind can unleash many positive things into your life, but you must have some knowledge how to use this. You must have some techniques to achieve the best results, otherwise you really can't reach your full potential.

There are different mental techniques you can try that will unlock the secrets to a successful life. Here are some of them:

Intuition

They say this is a natural born instinct. Some people claim that intuition is more commonly strong among females. Though there are some truths to these sayings, there are still some people with greater intuition than others. This kind of intuition is the power of the mind to perceive and send alarm signals to what may happen next. Intuition gives you a strong sense of conviction and a compelling force that is displayed through your "gut feel" or "suspicions." Intuition may especially benefit you when you are trying to make crucial decisions. When you try to develop this ability further, you can definitely sore through greater heights in life.

Telepathy

Some people say this is mind reading, but this is actually a way for two minds to communicate without saying words or using sign languages. Not all people can do this. It takes great skill and focus in order to be successful at it. If not careful, this could be a source of evil deeds, however, what most people take for granted is that this can also put into good use.

If you try to improve your powers of mental telepathy, you will be able to gain valuable insights into other people's thoughts and way of thinking. This could advance your career or help you deal with other people better. This also has the potential to improve your relationships and your transactions.

Clairvoyance

This is a mind technique that allows you to see things that you don't normally see using your five senses. It is also more commonly known as Extrasensory Perception or E.S.P. People who use this technique can see the image of an incident in their heads only to be described later by another person as an actual occurrence. This mind power is often useful to helping other people find their missing loved ones or by preventing some accident from happening.

Attraction

This has been an age-old law being practiced even in the ancient times. This technique helps you achieve success, prosperity and love by simply following the law of attraction. The methods involve in this law include positive thinking, visualization and affirmation. You allow yourself to think that the success, money and love will come to you when you visualize yourself in that position. There are so much more ways to unleash the power of the mind but these are the basic techniques that would help just about any person. You need to practice meditation as you try to master these techniques. Practice and training will also help you achieve what you want to achieve with these techniques.

BRAIN POWER

The brain is some sort of a main computer that controls all the functions of the human body. It basically controls human thoughts, feelings and memory. It consists of three major parts namely; the forebrain, hindbrain and the midbrain. The forebrain is home to the cerebrum, which is the source of intelligence, personality, emotion, and memory. On the other hand, the hindbrain contains the cerebellum; an organ that enhances bodily coordination, movement, and balance. The midbrain ensures coordination of messages to and from the brain.

Human brains need constant exercises to keep them up to the task of their functions. There are a number of activities people could engage in to increase brain power. Meditation is one such way people can enhance the capacities of their brains. This entails closing the eyes and paying keen detail to the breathing movements. Moreover, this activity demands that people should relax their muscles and let their minds wander. Meditation helps to clear the mind and ready the individual for any mental task.

Learning a foreign language also assists to increase brain power. This strategy could work well for those people in their old ages. Usually, such individuals face a decline in the brain function in line with their ages. Taking on new languages stimulates the brain by inducting new concepts into the mind. Thus, humans could be able to look at things in different ways by virtue of language differences. People who are fans of Mozart also have a head-start with regards to stimulated brains. A University of California-based study has indeed discovered that children who feature in chorus or piano lessons are adept at solving puzzles. Consequently, these children excelled at test like spatial intelligence and IQ tests.

Engaging in crossword puzzles is also beneficial in charging up the brain power. This activity could be a pastime, which would put the brain to task. This would in turn stimulate it into activity thereby keeping it busy. Sleep is also an integral task in increasing brain power. The human brain uses a lot of energy to fulfill its functions. Sleep serves to recharge the brain and prepares it for the next mental task. Ideally, human beings should aim for a minimum of five hours of sleep. Physical exercises are another important tip for people who need increase brain power. In this regard, certain exercises like walking or jogging helps to accentuate cognitive functions of the brain.

A powerful brain also requires that humans must develop healthy eating habits. There are numerous foods, which work to stimulate the functions of the brain. For instance, foods rich in folic acid increase the speed of information processing. Folic acid also helps to generate new cells as part of the production of DNAs. An increased blood flow in the brain is pivotal in enhancing an increase of the brain power. Chocolates are the perfect foods to accentuate the flow of blood in the brain. It assists in increasing learning capabilities and concentration levels.

Maximizing Brain Power to Achieve Greatness in Life

Most people believe that their brain power gets diminished as they grow older. They believe that the culprit is age when they start being forgetful and experience memory loss, but this cannot be further from the truth. Actually, one can do many things to keep their brain sharp and functioning at its peak to the end. There are many ways you can enhance and maximize your brain with help from brainwave entrainment technology.

- Exercise your brain. Reduced brain power is a result of one not exercising it enough. The brain, like any other muscle in the body needs its exercise in order to grow and become strong. One can easily do this by making sure they read every day. They should read widely from newspapers to novels to magazines. By forcing one's brain to learn new things every day and struggle to store all these new information, you keep it sharp. As they say, if you do not use it, you will lose it. A brain that is not properly utilized loses its power.
- One should exercise regularly. Physical exercise encourages growth of new brain cells. The brain also is exercised in the process making it stronger to hold new information from learning.
- Interacting socially with others sharpens one's brain and increases its power. This is because one learns new things when they spend time with others and keeps their brain active.
- One should keep their brain challenged by using puzzles, games, brainteasers and the like. These activities stimulate the brain and work it out. These activities will ensure they keep mental illness at bay.
- One should endeavor to sleep well by getting enough sleep every day. Plenty of rest is crucial for a healthy mind and body. Your mind is at its sharpest after it has just rested. Sleeping two hours only a day will make one sleepy and tired the next day. This makes them lose focus.
- One needs to manage his stress levels. Reducing ones stress will help keep your mind sharp. If you accumulate a lot of stress and

you do not work it manage it, your brain gets crowded with it and loses its strength.

- One should eat properly. A good balanced diet not only keeps one's body in trim shape, but it also keeps the mind functioning properly. This is because healthy food fuels the mind and keeps it working in peak condition.
- One should follow a different routine sometimes to grow their brain power. Following the same routine each time you do something denies your mind challenges. Challenges keep the mind sharp and focused. One should follow a different route to work or change the type of music you listen to. Your brain will be fit and alert each time you do something differently.
- One should sharpen their senses by doing something with some of their senses shut off. Eat with eyes closed for example. Doing this will force one's mind to concentrate more and in the process sharpens the mind.
- One should use nutrient supplements that give ones mind the power and energy it needs to stay strong and sharp. The supplements also help to keep forgetfulness and other mental problems at bay. People with maximized brain power from brainwave entrainment technology and the above tips can achieve anything they set their minds to achieve.

Which Foods Keep Your Brain Working Well?

Thanks to all the pressures of modern living, we all discover that from time to time, we are often too tired or stressed to think. Nevertheless, this may not be the case since there are varieties of readily available spices, drinks, and foods that we can consume, not only to boost or energize our memory and help us focus, but also to delay or reverse the onset of debilitating diseases which affect the brain such as the Alzheimer's Disease.

Sometimes we all lose interest or focus in whatever we are doing due to stress or fatigue. By good luck, there are some supplements or foods that can improve focus, memory, and concentration, in accordance with the recent research by the World Health Organization (WHO). If you combine and mix these 'brain foods' with daily exercise, good night's sleep and good hydration, you could significantly boost your brain power. So if you are searching for ways to boost your memory, enhance concentration and stay focused, you can check out these simple and readily available foods that will make you smarter like Einstein in no time.

Apples

Apples are the king of fruits and they are also known for the brain food. They are one of the foods that scientists say will contribute to overall good health, help you to think clearly and of course, boost your memory. We all know the old saying, 'an apple a day keeps the doctor away' and 'you are what you eat' which certainly stills holds true even today. So what makes the apple the top of this list? Well, they contain a certain group of compounds and nutrients such as pectin which are fiber, quercetin which protects and boosts memory, riboflavin which produces energy and lastly polyphenol which are strong antioxidants. These compounds help to protect the brain from the kind of damage that cause neuro degenerative diseases such as Parkinson's and Alzheimer's. Not only do they have brain power but they also help to lower blood cholesterol levels, build strong teeth and prevent the oxidation of bad LDL cholesterol (a chemical process that turns it into an artery clogging plague). They also decrease the risk of liver, lung, colon, breast and other cancer as well as asthma and heart disease.What a wonderful fruit! Also, make sure that you eat the peel as the apple skin has 2 to 6 times the antioxidants as the flesh.Cherries, oysters, berries and even curry also have a high rank among foods that can help boost your brain, promote heart health and give you energy.

Chocolate

Today chocolate is considered an anti flammatory, anti aging 'superfood' for both the brain and the body. But how does this lenient treat live up to its plug? Eating amounts of dark chocolate is guaranteed to have many health benefits as they assist the brain to release chemicals known as endorphins (which help the brain to function much better). The studies examining the health benefit of chocolate continue to show new and appealing benefits of chocolate, especially in the realms of mood, cognitive function, and heart or blood vessel health. Also, eating chocolate can improve anxiety and depression symptoms and help improve feelings of contentedness. If you consume the right kinds of chocolate every day, they can help to keep your mind sharp and alert, keep your cardiovascular pumping and keep your mood happy and calm. For instance, cocoa chocolate and dark chocolate are best known to boost attention, working memory speed, brain processing speed and speech fluency (even to the elderly). These chocolates are a rich source of flavanols, which are compounds that boost the brain activity and enhance mood effects as well. You can eat as little as a third chocolate per day to increase the blood flow to your brain and also protect yourself against age related issues such as memory loss.

Eggs

According to the latest news in nutrition, eggs are now back from exile just on time to help the aging America from memory loss. Eggs, and especially the yolk, have received a lot of attention with controversy over their cholesterol content. So how do eggs actually help to boost the memory? Well, as it turns out, eggs are packed with choline, that your brain converts to acetylcholine (a neurotransmitter that assists the brain cells to keep the memories intact and communicates with each other). With less than 80 calories each, eggs are comparatively loaded with protein and they have a low calorie. Eggs are also packed with cholesterol which made them end up on the 'bad for you' list in the first place over the past few decades.One York has 200 mg of cholesterol, and for many years, it was believed that dietary cholesterol was the major contributor and cause of heart disease. But it appears that it was mistaken much like the tenacious myth that skims milk is much healthier than whole milk. Eggs contain many nutritive elements that your brain and other body cells need every day. They are rich in choline, vitamin B12, and folate which is good for boosting g your memory.

Water

Your body was designed to work in a specific way just like any other machine that has specific instructions about what it requires and how to keep it operating optimally. Over 70 per cent of your body is made of water and every function in the body depend on the water including the activities of the nervous system and the brain. Your body is also composed of a delicate balance of minerals, electrons, and organic compounds most of which are supplied through the water that you drink. Therefore, it is proven that if you're not well hydrated, it can affect your focus, cause headaches, lead to memory loss, cause depression, sleeping problems, anger issues and brain fatigue. Drinking water provides your brain with enough electrical energy for all the brain functions including memory processes. You will also be able to think fast, be more focused, experience great creativity and clarity and even reduce the risk of neurotransmitter diseases. It is quite easy to integrate a few supplements or foods that will enhance your memory and focus in your daily diet. You can take an egg in the morning, a cup of green tea after lunch, some curry in your spaghetti sauce at supper time and a lot of water to keep the brain working well.

Cinnamon

Did you know that cinnamon was worth more than gold to the ancient Egyptians? This is mostly because cinnamon was long believed to have healthy and medicinal properties which made it extremely valuable. There are thousands of man made supplements, food products and chemically manufactured tablets that claim to increase or boost brain power but none of these offers the delicious, tasty flavor cinnamon does. Even today, cinnamon is still one of the most consumed and used products in the world. It is a sweet smelling spice that has been found to boost and energize brain activity and help to relieve memory loss and nervous tension. Cinnamon is also a safe and tasty method to slow down the aging process. Chewing cinnamon flavored gum or just smelling it can help to improve and enhance the cognitive process. It also contains a chemical compound known as sodium benzoate which is used to treat neural disorders. Cinnamon has 3 active compounds which make it so nutritious such as the Cinnamaldehyde, cinnamyl alcohol, and cinnamyl acetate. It also contains a flavonol range and other antioxidants along with a remarkable amount of fiber, calcium, and manganese. These compounds have proved to boost memory, curb food cravings, reverse or delay cognitive impairment and benefit Alzheimer's, Parkinson's and diabetic patients. Cinnamon is indeed nature's wonder spice.

Coffee

Coffee is the planets most single valuable traded food commodity with more than 2 billion cups enjoyed worldwide daily. It's effectiveness as a high-performance brain fuel continues to make it liquid gold and it is not surprising that it's main active ingredient is caffeine. Coffee helps you to wake up in the mornings and keeps you active throughout the day. So how does this magic ingredient help boost your brain? Well, as the caffeine hits the brain it suppresses a neurotransmitter known as adenosine, which influences alertness, concentration, and attention. It works up on your brain during the day just like a mercury rising in the thermometer. Caffeine also stimulates brain chemicals such as dopamine and glutamate which helps and gives you an energy surge, improve your mental performance and slows down the age related mental decline. It also increases serotonin (a major mood influencer) and improves learning up to 10 percent. Caffeine has even proved to relieve headaches and migraines, benefit Alzheimer's, Parkinson's and type 2 diabetic patients. There is also a downside to coffee since caffeine can affect sleep patterns and evidence also suggests that there's an association between daily intake of caffeine, day time sleepiness and sleep quality.Coffee is truly a perfect method to energize and boost your brain.

Oily Fish

No doubt you have possibly heard that eating fish can make you smarter, which to some extent is completely true. Eating oily fish that are high in the essential omega 3 or fatty acids such as salmon, trout, sardines tilapia and other fish can help to boost the brain. Fatty acids that are found in fish and seafood are crucial components of our brain cells and they improve learning strength and memory function by up to 15 per cent. Studies show that eating food rich in omega 3 can boost the blood flow of the brain, improve the performance of mental tasks and reduce the risks of suffering from neurotransmitter diseases such as Alzheimer's and dementia. Also by eating oily fish, you can increase your brain size in later life and also help to prevent age related mental decline. Fish have added the benefit of containing the nutrient choline (a chemical which is essential for memory). Since the solid (non-water) part of your brain is composed of fat, you must provide it with 'good fats' or the essential fatty acids through your diet because the body doesn't produce them. Fish is really an amazing brain food.

Iron

Iron deficiency is the most common condition that is often linked to numerous adverse effects like diminished intelligence, short attention span and difficulty in concentrating. Iron is a required nutrient for it the production of hemoglobin (the component in red blood cells that carries oxygen and delivers it to the tissues). If iron becomes deficient in your body, hemoglobin levels can fail and then cause anemia. Iron also participates in the making of the brain chemicals (neurotransmitters) like dopamine and serine which have broadly advantageous effects on the brain function and mood as well. An easy blood test is conducted to determine whether you have iron deficiency. Study shows that adult women require 18 mg of iron every day, post menopausal women and men require 8 mg every day. Adding more iron rich foods will not automatically boost your brain power, but being even mildly deficient in iron could negatively impact memory, learning, and attention span. Chicken livers are on offer the top sources of food that is rich in iron, with 12.8mg per 3 - ounce serving. Even though they are high in cholesterol, they are comparatively low in saturated fat. Other sources of food that are rich in iron are oysters (with nearly 10 mg per dozen) and the lean beef (with 6 mg per ounces). Also beans, vitamin C and iron fortified cereals help the body to absorb iron.

Blackberries

If you want to slow down your ageing process and also preserve your brain's activity and vitality, the secret to doing so is by taking blackberries. These juicy and delicious berries have a phenomenal anti oxidant properties which boost your brain power and nourish your body. They contain high amounts of ellagic acid and garlic acid, a well known chemo preventative (with anti bacterial and anti viral properties). They are also rich in fiber and vitamin C which have been shown to help decrease the risks of certain cancers. They have low carbohydrates, calories (70 calories per cup)and they have no fat. This means that you can take a lot of this stupendous fruit without having the guilt or sabotaging you weight loss target or objectives. These taste and delicious fruit contains several micro nutrients which work wonders on your body. Blackberries are indeed an amazing superfruit.

Spinach

A single bunch of spinach can perform wonders for your brain. Spinach was long promoted as the food which gave Popeye his convex muscles. Spinach is loaded with antioxidants which scientists say could block the effects of the free radicals, toxins produced by the body which damage cells and cause cancer, strokes and heart disease. It is also a great source of folate and a kind of vitamin K and vitamin E which help to boost the brain memory. It contains flavonoids that act as potent antioxidants which slow the effects of aging on the brain. It also boosts learning capacity and motor skills. A few leaves of cooked spinach loads a third of foliate and 5 times the amount of Vitamin K that you require in a day. Maybe this is why a neurology study in 2006 reveals that eating three plates of leafy-green, cruciferous and yellow vegetables a day can reverse or delay cognitive decline by 40 percent. Spinach has not only proved to help the brain but it also gives a knock-out punch to cancer and it even protects and improves eyesight. Spinach is packed with high-quality nutrition enough to make you feel like the bulging Popeye.

Grape Juice

Grape juice contains protein, fiber, copper, iron, potassium, folate vitamins A, K, C and B2. They are also rich in polyphenols and natural sugar, which must be consumed in moderation. Therefore, including a glass of tasty grape juice in your daily diet might just boost your memory and your brain performance. It also helps those who live a stressful lifestyle like working mothers. Studies show that by adding a glass of grape juice (especially concord grape juice) to the daily diet might boost memory function and performance of highly stressed people and even in elder people with mild declines of memory. Concord grape juice is a rich and good source of polyphenols and potent antioxidants which mop up or clear harmful reactive species of oxygen which have been recognized as the key to the ageing process. So by consuming or adding concord grape juice to your daily diet for about three months you may boost your spatial memory and drive performance. Grape juice not only helps to boosts your memory but it also protects you from cancer, lowers bad cholesterol, improves cardiovascular health, fights fatigue and it improves eyesight. It is also evident that grape juice also has a long term effect which can allow you to consistently maintain a better performance even when you have stopped drinking it.

Boost Your Brain Power Using Neurobics

Neurons refer to nerve cells found in the human brain. Neurobiologists highly recommend neurobics as the most appropriate exercise to boost your brain power. The habits you are currently used to are responsible for your current results. You can also improve or better your results if you change your habits. There are several ways to boost your brain power which people can employ and get desirable outcomes. However, this book intends to highlight only the major strategies that can be used by different ages to boost brain power. All the strategies that are discussed here are in form of exercises:

Stimulating other senses.

Just like the first strategy, try to do things differently. For instance, closing your eyes when carrying out ordinary activities such as taking a bath, dressing, washing dishes will ignite and develop dormant senses that you rarely use in the course of your daily activities. For instance, blind people have a superior auditory sense as compared to people with acute eyesight. Blind people also have a sharp sense of touch and smell and can identify people they regularly interact with just by touching them or smelling them. Boosting brain power requires more than just carrying out the ordinary activities.

Developing motor pathways.

This is an essential exercise recommended for people in all ages. Even at old age, you can employ this exercise to boost your brain power. Tightening up connections as well as new pathways is quite simple so long as a person is consistent in the exercise. For the right-handed, try using your left hand when changing clothes, making phone

69

calls, eating, writing among other activities that you perform using your right hand. This exercise helps in creating new pathways for nerves and aids to boost your brain power.

Having enough sleep and rest.

It is recommended that sleeping for eight hours in the 24-hour cycle will greatly boost your brain power. Lack of enough sleep and rest leads to a feeling of stress. The lesser the stress, the more your mental functioning will be. The current economic hardships have seen people spending as little 3 hours on sleep to make ends meet. Beware, such habits will have adverse effects on the functionality of your brain which you need for the success of your chores.

Cognitive ability.

This might involve playing your favorite game or doing any other activity that will task your mind. For instance, use a new way to reach the workplace such as using a new path, traveling different directions, changing the position you sit in an office or using a different chair, disarranging the contents of your table among other adjustments in your daily routine. This is where brainwave entrainment technology comes in, such as watching a new movie on the latest DVD. Such movies require extra thinking hence boost your brain power. Stagnation in habits bars the growth and development of your brain. If you are used to watching soaps, try watching horror movies and your brain will definitely be ignited.

TIPS TO BOOST YOUR BRAIN POWER

Do you ever check in with your brain to determine if it needs a tune-up? Just like the oil in a car, routine maintenance helps dust off the debris collected so your brain can run at its top intellectual performance.

Do you take time to evaluate your routine bi-weekly, bi-monthly, or bi-yearly?

Does your body feel connected to your brain? If so, when and for how long?

By defining these questions for yourself, you can start to break down the clots that are clouding clarity in the mind. When the brain is vibrant, active and stimulated the body follows in sequence.

Our brains have the capacity to change.

We call this brain plasticity or neuroplasticity. Meaning the life of the brain has the ability to be altered at any stage from childhood to adulthood. Microscopic changes in an individual's neurons can remap themselves in areas of healthy development, learning, memory, and recovery.

All you need to do is invest some time and effort into regular training for your brain. It can be simple, and you don't need to be a genius to master these tune-ups.

By creating a reset for the brain to run at full capacity, one can awaken the mind to its fullest expression. By the brain's activity normalizing, the routine one experiences daily become less mundane, needs less stimulation to produce positive energy force and clarity becomes the key feature.

Do you want to discover some tips that help boost your brain power?

Exercise.

We all know that we should be getting regular exercise. However, most entrepreneur lead busy, rushed lives, and can't always find the time to fit physical activity in. The trick might be to think of it in reverse: you can't afford not to exercise if you want to live a long, healthy, productive life.

Exercise not only benefits your brain health and cognition, it can also improve your memory. In the long run, it can even protect your brain against degeneration. If that isn't reason enough to get into a regular workout routine, who knows what is?

Reading

What books have you read lately? Reading relieves tension and stress. It also offers new information which plays on your curiosity and expands the mind. The best part about reading is it trains your mind to use your imagination. It forces your brain to imagine what you are reading. It is improving your creativity while stimulating and adapting to new ideas and knowledge. The more you read the more you can visualize using your imagination.

Drink coffee.

Many people start their days with a cup of coffee, and it turns out this ritual could actually benefit your cognitive functions in the short term.

Caffeine, of course, helps to keep you alert. However, it can also help you to stay focused on repetitive and tedious tasks, and will even boost your intelligence, including your reaction time and reasoning.

Obviously, the effects of coffee are not permanent. However, it can make your brain work more efficiently until that caffeine high wears off.

Play with more puzzles and other mind-boggling games

Have you ever wondered why you see so many adults playing puzzles? Well, what you may not know is that puzzles are extremely great for the brain and the mind. Believe it or not, Doctors even recommend to adults that struggle with focusing to play video games or puzzles for a few minutes each day to regain more focus. It helps bring your mind to new heights by making you think larger and bigger, and digging deep to find the solved pieces. These puzzles can be played both online or offline, and they are great to do for exercising your head no matter where you are.

Aside from simply puzzles where you create the whole picture, you should consider doing word puzzles as well because of the increased thinking in your head. Word puzzles are wonderful to play because it gets your mind going and actually thinking what the clues mean. These can usually be found on newspapers and online as well. You should also consider playing crossword puzzles, as they can help tremendously with exercising your thinking and eye-coordination. Thus, increasing your brain power to a huge extent. So, you can be sure that these will help you out a lot with your brain.

Sleep at the right time and create a schedule

By sleeping at the right time and creating a real schedule, you can be sure that your mind and brain will be more alert during the times when you need it most. Some people tend to fall asleep at different times, and then they end up waking up at different times, causing for them to struggle a lot with being productive throughout the day. Productivity is of the essence for some people, especially those who want to achieve the most success possible.

People who create schedules are not only more productive and are more organized, but also are people who know what's going on because of the fact that their mind is in the right place the way it's supposed to be. Sleeping the minimum 8 hours can be helpful, and as long as you are able to set a perfect time to sleep and wake up, you can expect for your mind to be in the right place at the right time.

Memory Training

How are you training your brain? What memory tools do you have in place to remember and attain information? Everybody wants a better memory, but how can you achieve this. If you start disciplining yourself to retain numbers, from phone to driver's licenses that is a start. Also adding memory focused games in your free time either from an app or sudoku's can help you improve your memory. In time, with discipline, you will improve your brain memory retention.

Curiosity

How curious are you? Start getting in the habit of being curious about everything from products and services to skills and techniques. By becoming more curious and questioning everything, you force your brain to innovate and create new ways of developing ideas. Curiosity is what the best inventors embodied, which is how you have things like electricity, and technology.

Limit External Device Reliance

If you are constantly relying on phones, computers, and calculators then you are limiting your ability to increase your brainpower. By being fixed to your devices you lose brain capacity to function without. Try to resist using your device all the time, you don't need it, instead try to use your natural gift for memory. The brain. It is a powerful tool, that can help you achieve greatness, but you either use it or lose it.

Get Some Sunlight.

Sunlight and exercise can sometimes go hand in hand. This mostly depends on what part of the world you live in, how much sunlight is available at different times of the year and how realistic it is for you to spend time in the outdoors.

Getting too little sunlight is not good for your brain. Higher levels of vitamin D in your system allow you to perform better, and can even slow down the aging of your brain.

Too much sunlight can be bad for your skin, but if you aren't getting enough, your brain functions may suffer. Of course, you can always take vitamin D supplements if you find that you aren't able to get outside as much as you would like to. Just remember to take supplements in moderation.

Build Strong Connections.

It has often been said that the entrepreneurial journey is a lonely one. As it turns out, that may not be good for your cognitive functions.

If you often feel lonely, it can actually result in psychological and cognitive decline, as these feelings can have a negative impact on your sleep, increase your blood pressure, contribute to depression and even lower your overall well-being.

Spontaneity

Experiencing something new actually stimulates the brain. It allows for the brain receptors to adapt and activate new neural pathways. By switching up your routine, you alleviate getting into a rut of your own patterns. By experiencing spontaneity you can change the structure of your brain while increasing your intelligence. So go mix it up—go to a new coffee shop, get out of the car and ride a bike, change your exercise routine, or go explore the great outdoors. The possibilities are endless, just motivate yourself to try something new.

Healthy Nutrition

What are you feeding your body these days? Your diet is a gigantic part of healthy brain functioning. Our brains consume about 20% of all of our nutrients. So try to eat healthy; fruits, dark green vegetables, grilled fish and chicken, beans and rice. Also try to take supplements if you are lacking certain nutrients and vitamins. This will ensure a healthy brain to function in your daily tasks.

Eat well.

It shouldn't come as a surprise that nutrition plays a significant part in your brain health. Entrepreneurs are often rushing from one meeting to another, leaving themselves with very little or no time to eat well.

You have to focus on getting the right kind of nutrition. Antioxidants and amino acids are particularly important, and vitamin E can also be beneficial. Drinking wine is known to improve your cognitive function -- assuming you consume it in moderation -- and nuts, blueberries, whole grains, and avocados are also beneficial. What's good for your body also tends to be good for your brain.

Spatial Relationships

How often do you rely on your digital devices to guide you to a location? Most likely a 90% chance, every trip. If you use paper maps it helps you identify with the spatial relationships surrounding you. It also helps you understand the general awareness of your surroundings. If you can go somewhere once, pay attention to your parameters, because most likely you will be able to train your brain to remember how to direct yourself anywhere.

Sleep Medicine

Sleep is the magic pill. Your brain cannot function properly without a certain amount of sleep. Sleeping between 9pm and midnight ensures the best quality of sleep. It regenerates your cells and resets the mind for the next day's activities. When you sleep you are also processing the information you learned the previous day, so you need as much sleep as possible to wake with a clean slate, which creates less stress and anxiety.

Regular Physical Conditioning

Regular exercise helps the brain function while eliminating brain fog. Exercise can also reduce both the biological and cognitive consequences of aging. Cool huh? With regular physical conditioning you can increase brain blood flow to the hippocampus, which is the key brain region affected by Alzheimer's disease. Therefore increasing cognitive memory. If you're not exercising, then a simple solution is to get started.

Positive Thinking

When you are positive your brain turns on a light. It reduces stress and anxiety which actually kills brain neurons and stops producing new ones. By creating positive thought patterns your brain cells increase rapidly and dramatically reduce stress and anxiety. So in essence, if you can reduce those negative thoughts patterns you can increase your amount of brain cells.

Practice Remembering Things

If you feel like your mind lacks some concentration, try to remember some things throughout your day. For example, try remembering your Mom or friends' phone number by looking at the pattern of the numbers. This can help a lot with your memory and overall brain power, as it can help keep your mind focused and deeply thinking about the numbers. Remember that it does take time to remember anything that you see, but as long as you really try to remember it to the best of your ability, you'll find your brain to start remembering things faster and faster the more that you exercise it.

The Art of Thinking Clearly

No amount of training will ever compensate for crystal clear thinking. This is not an ability that we are born with, we have to study the concept and then commit to working at it.

The first step to clear thinking is to clear away any emotions, m bias, trivia and preconceived notions that you have regarding the decision that you are about to make. Concentrate on the information that essential to making the right decision.

Facilitate your clear thinking process by using these lesson:

Round Up More Than The Usual Suspects.

Get down and dirty with the research that you need to do and assemble all of the facts. You are going to get better data by asking better questions. Clear thinking is facilitated by observation and a willingness to look beyond the obvious.

Drop Your Musts.

We all have a tendency to turn our major desires into must haves. This, however, limits your ability to think objectively. The key to clear thinking is to remain flexible.

Take A Knife To The Big Decisions.

You wouldn't want to try to swallow a steak whole and you should not try to take a large problem and tackle it full on. You can chunk the bigger problem down to smaller problems and tackle those in succession until you have dominated the larger issue.

Look For Hidden Opportunities.

When trying to make a decision many of us get stuck in either/or scenarios. Move beyond those and think about as many alternative forms of action that you can imagine. Each time you think of another avenue, see if you can think of at least one more. This will give you more choices when it comes to making your final decision.

Become An Amiable Skeptic.

View things with a critical eye. Reserve judgment if you feel that you are being moved in any one direction against your will. The ability to think clearly requires that you maintain your skepticism, but you don't want to move the decision making process into an adversarial arena; so, have fun with it.

Create A Balance Sheet.

Take a pen and paper and write down all of the options that you have come up with during your research. List all of the advantages and disadvantages of each option and rate each one on a scale to 1 to 10. One of the major components of clarity of thought is that you remove emotion from the decision making process and this quantification of the options allows you to do just that.

Use Confidence To Keep Your Cool.

Stand back and look at all of the good decisions that you have made in the past. Clear thinking requires you to have trust in yourself and in your decisions no matter what mistakes you have made in the past.

Tips to the Art of Thinking

Getting what you want is, in actuality, the result of an equation as simple as this. It may sound too easy or unbelievable, but that's probably only because you have never broken it down to truly get an idea of what it takes to reach your desired goal.

Ever known someone who seemed to be able to think themselves into not being sick? Some people really have mastered the art of making their thoughts work for them, instead of against them. Because, on the other hand, there are people who seem to think themselves into being sick. It just goes to show the power of our thoughts. How we think and the energy we put into making these thoughts our reality.

Honestly, the problem is often that people do not include all of the three main components to arrive at the desired outcome. Having desire and belief without putting any action behind it does not lead to the right solution. Just one of those two plus action still will not get that exact result, either. So, now that you see the equations that can result in getting what you want or reaching your goal, it is time to understand how the way in which you think can help you live in a manner that desire, belief and action equal your goal or to get you what you want.

The Power of Thinking

Using positive thinking can improve your life and help change your life completely. The idea is to begin to use positive thinking as part of your natural thought process. Using positive thinking, help determine your desire. This can be more than one thing. Usually, this is the easiest part of the process.

You will have put into play the power of belief. This means believing with your entire heart and mind that you can do this: You can achieve the goals and get what you want and desire. Belief can also be what falters though, if not careful. You will have moments of doubt; that is normal. The key is to not get hung up on self-doubt, but move back towards believing in what you can achieve.

Actions Speak Louder Than Words

One of the most vital parts of this process is action. Desiring and believing we do with our minds. Now, it is time to put the effort into making things fall into place and work out to reach your goals. So, with organization and proper planning, the key to success is to use daily action to make things happen.

Daily action means that you are putting real effort into making things happen each and every day. You cannot want something and just hope it happens without using any energy to make it happen. On the other hand, if you invest real effort into making things happen you can almost be guaranteed that you will reach your goals.

Smaller Goals

Use smaller goals along the way to track your progress. These small goals will lead up to your bigger ones. They will also help you to feel as though you are having some success. If you only have that one main goal in place, it can begin to seem impossible you will get there. A cross country drive unfolds one mile at a time. You wouldn't want to miss the milestones along the way by being only focused on the destination that is still down the road a way.

Getting What You Want

There's another formula, or method, to use as you approach the process of using positive thinking to obtain your goals and get what you want. The first thing you have to do is define it. Make it specific, not vague. Instead of just "I want to be a millionaire," define it as "I want to be an entrepreneur who owns my own home-based business and is successful enough to become an automatic millionaire."

Write it out. When something goes from head to paper, it becomes more of a reality. This is you writing out your goals, not just settling for a vague thought. Once you have your goals written out, take some time to refine them even more. This may mean breaking one goal into smaller goals or getting even more specific.

Give your dreams, plans and goals realism by speaking them into truth. Speak of these things as if they are your present reality. "I am that successful entrepreneur with my own home-based business." "I am on my way to becoming a millionaire." The most important part, and also the best part, is to be grateful.

Show and express gratitude for this new life you are providing for yourself. Be grateful for giving yourself the opportunity to fire your boss and make a new and improved life for yourself, and your family. Even if being a millionaire isn't your reality yet, be grateful that it is now even a possibility. This helps you retain a positive outlook and be grateful for everything along the way. Be grateful for the little things as well as the big ones.

Keep in Mind...

All these things you are learning about how to be better as a leader, an entrepreneur, a goal setter, a dreamer and a person, in general, are bits of knowledge you are arming yourself with. But, remember, self-knowledge does no good unless it turns into self-action. Your thoughts are only that until you cause them to develop by using effort, energy and action.

Thinking Habits of the Mega Successful

Self-defeating thoughts can derail a career whether it's leadership, selling, entrepreneurship... you name it. Wildly successful individuals leave clues from which we can benefit. To reach your career goals, adopt the mindset of the top 5%.

Develop these thinking habits to advance your career:

Integrative Processing

They have the cognitive ability to break down each problem into manageable pieces and discern which are the critical components. They can assimilate all the variables of a situation into a single homogeneous image and then use this understanding to make decisions regarding planning, resource allocation, and solving problems.

Personal Accountability

This thinking habit prevents making excuses for a bad decision. The superstar's brain enables them to be transparent with themselves. They will make every effort to try and identify the cause of that bad decision. Their focus is more on correcting the problem to ensure future success than on protecting themselves from other people's opinions.

Self-Belief

Their mind communicates success. They visualize succeeding at each step of plan. For example, a superstar salesperson believes in their ability to execute the sales process--prospecting, building trust, qualifying, analyzing needs, presenting solutions, negotiation, closing sales, etc. They believe in their abilities with accuracy. Their mind is absolutely convinced they will succeed--regardless if the prospect buys or not.

Emotional Distance

Mega successful people can remain emotionally neutral (unaffected) by positive or negative experiences with others. Their mind does not internalize flattery or rejection. They are indifferent to surface level emotions directed at them. Instead, they focus their attention on the mission, following their plan, listening, learning and problem solving.

Initiative

The super successful are self-starters. They wait for no one and they have no need for a cattle prod. Their minds crystallize their vision and they are emotionally connected to it. They are self-motivated to initiate each activity. They intuitively adapt to difficult situations and navigate around unforeseen obstacles without waiting for supervisory instruction.

Ways to Be a Better Thinker

Here are some principles of better thinking that you can apply to get more from your mind, every day.

Find a quiet place

Noise can quickly break your train of thought. Find a quiet place where you'll be less likely to encounter interruptions. Remove any visual distractions, like clutter. If you're having difficulty locating a place where you can sit quietly, think about finding a better time to think as opposed to a better place. Try getting to work before your co-workers so you can avoid the hustle and bustle of the day.

Reduce stress

It's hard to think clearly when you're a ball of stress. Anxiety has a way of causing your mind to flit from thought to thought or just freeze up altogether. Find ways to relax and recharge. Meditation is one way to quiet your mind and recalibrate your thoughts. It's important to pay attention to your emotions so you can approach your tasks with clarity.

"Emotions are a gift to us, and critical thinking strongly depends on our emotional awareness and how we deal with it. We should always systematically and automatically ask ourselves what is our thinking that led to this certain emotion," says Christ Lewis in Critical Thinking.

Go outside

Take a walk and enjoy the fresh air so you can clear your head. Sometimes, a change of scenery is all you need to get your thought process going. Besides, sitting indoors all day isn't good for your mind or your body.

Go ahead and daydream.

Forget efficiency. Scientists have discovered that daydreaming is an important tool for creativity: It causes a rush of activity in a circuit known as the default network, which connects different parts of the brain and allows the mind to make new associations. The daydreaming brain is actually in overdrive.

Don't be afraid to make a mistake

One way you can unintentionally block your thought process is to become fearful of making an error. This will lead you to overthink the problem or task at hand. In order to come to the best conclusion, you need to try to stop yourself from worrying about the outcome.

"Fail to succeed. Intentionally get it wrong to inevitably get it even more right. Mistakes are great teachers — they highlight unforeseen opportunities and holes in your understanding," says authors Edward B. Burger and Michael Starbird

Think about thinking.

Metacognition, as this is known, is a crucial skill. Many scientists argue that the best predictor of good judgment isn't intelligence or experience; it's the willingness to engage in introspection. The brain is like a Swiss Army Knife, full of different tools. When picking out a couch, we can trust our emotions, but we should rely on the rational brain when scrutinizing the fine print of a mortgage. Unless you think about which mental tool is best suited for the task at hand, you could end up flustered, even sweating, in the sofa aisle at Ikea.

Tap your emotions.

Our conscious thoughts are only a fraction of what's going on in our brains. At any given moment, the unconscious is taking in vast amounts of information that we're not even aware of and processing it all very quickly. Based on its conclusions, the brain generates emotions. So don't disregard that subtle feeling telling you to avoid the salmon special. Your personal supercomputer is trying to tell you something.

Don't make a decision under pressure

One of the worst things you can do is try to make an important decision while you're being pressured for an answer. It's hard to be clear and thoughtful when someone is waiting on you to respond immediately. If possible, tell him or her you need some time to think things through and that you'll return with an answer by a specific deadline.

Challenge yourself

Those who consistently put their brain to work have an easier time solving complex problems. Exercise your brain by reading on a regular basis or completing tasks that require critical thinking skills. Remain curious and hungry to learn something new every chance you get.

Burger and Starbird advocate continuing to challenge yourself beyond your formal education: "Education does not stop with the end of your formal schooling. Even if your formal school days are long past, you are a still a student and, hopefully, will always be one."

Be skeptical of your memories.

In recent years, scientists have demonstrated that human memories are surprisingly dishonest. The act of recalling an event (say, your eighth birthday party) changes the structure of that memory in the brain. Details are tweaked; the narrative is altered. The more you think about it, the less accurate your recollection becomes, and the less reliable it is as a basis for making any kind of conclusion. (So maybe you shouldn't hire a clown for your kid's party after all.)

Don't expect to diet and finish the crossword.

It turns out that the prefrontal cortex, the area of the brain responsible for willpower and cognitive thought, is a rather feeble bit of flesh and easily depleted. In a telling study, people who were asked to remember a seven-digit number and then offered a snack were much more likely to choose chocolate cake over fruit salad than were those who were asked to remember a one-digit number. The first group's self-control "muscles" were exhausted! It's important to realize that you can do everything—just not all at once.

Consider alternative points of view.

Professional poker players often use a simple trick when they suspect another player of bluffing: They think about how the player would act if he or she weren't bluffing. The brain naturally filters the world to confirm what it already believes (which is why conservatives watch Fox News and liberals watch MSNBC). But this habit is limiting and dangerous; you could be fixating on the wrong answers.

Challenge your preferences.

Like presumptive beliefs, your supposed likes and dislikes can limit your mind. I used to be a bit of an expensive-wine snob. But then I did a blind taste test of wines from different price ranges and discovered what scientists have since confirmed: There is no correlation between the price of a bottle and how much you'll enjoy it. By figuring out what you truly like—be it cheap wine or fancy shoes—you can enjoy life, not to mention spend more wisely.

Take long showers.

Studies show that moments of insight often arrive when you're not aware that you're thinking of the problem, such as during a warm shower or a long stroll. This is because insights are typically generated by a rush of high-frequency gamma-band neural activity in the brain's right hemisphere, and a mind is better able to tune in to that hemisphere when it is stress-free.

Study your mistakes.

One common trait of successful people is their willingness to focus on their fumbles. Even when they do well, they insist on looking at what they could have done better. Such perfectionism might not be a recipe for happiness, but it's a vital component of learning, since brain cells figure out how to get things right by analyzing what they got wrong.

The Lost Art of Thinking

"Direct your thoughts, control your emotions, and ordain your destiny." - Napoleon Hill

Never before in history has the average person had access to so much information. You are often just a few clicks away from the answer to almost any question you may have. We do not even have to be in one location to access information because of the wonder of the smart phone. And yet, people know less and think less for themselves than before. We have become intellectually lazy and believe what we are told rather than find things out for ourselves. There is a lot of information out there, but very little knowledge.

Success-minded people are people who think. They do not limit their thoughts to popular opinion or the realm of what is possible but rather are willing to stand alone and think of the impossible. William Arthur Ward, one of America's most quoted authors, said, "Nothing limits achievement like small thinking; nothing expands possibilities like unleashed thinking." There are really no limits to what can be done and achieved by those who are willing to think.

The challenge in our world today is that thinking is seemed as dangerous, risky and difficult. It is dangerous because those who think are more difficult to control. If you do not think that others, especially the government, want to control you then you are not thinking at all. Every day we are told what to believe and how we are to act. Forget what we know is true, what we can discover for ourselves or even common sense, we are to believe that we are told to believe.

Another way this is played out is in the education system. They academics of the day have been dumb down over the years. Out of a foolish idea that "everyone should be a winner" and never wanting to place one person over another, the standards have been lower and those who would have excelled are discouraged and even punished.

Add to this the fact that thinking is just out of fashion any more. If you tell someone that you are taking time just to think, they think you are odd or wasting time. Ralph Waldo Emerson was right when he said, "In this world, if a man sits down to think, he is immediately asked if he has a headache."

"A person should think like a man of action - act like a man of thought." - Henri-Louis Bergson

What does it mean to think? What must a success-minded person do to be a thinking person? I believe these questions are best answered by another question: What is it that thinking people do that others do not do? I will answer this with only five of the many actions that are taken by thinking people.

Thinkers Think For Themselves

Many people like to think that they are thinking for themselves but in reality they are not. They are basing their opinions and thought on the information that others have given them. This is not saying all that information is wrong, it is just unquestioned. Unquestioned information is not only dangerous but also foolish. It is like saying, "I saw it on the internet, therefore it must be true."

We believe blindly the things we are told for a number of reasons. They can be good reasons like we respect the person telling us as an authority and we believe they are honest and trustworthy. In those cases they can be believed, but you still need to think about what they are saying. Other times we may be believing someone just because we like them or we like how they look. Some of the most successful manipulators and deceivers of all time have been some of the best liked people. They were able to charm their way into people's minds and get them to believe some of the most outrageous things.

Oscar Wilde once said, "A man who does not think for himself does not think at all." When we allow others to do our thinking for us, no matter how much we trust them or how intelligent they may appear, we give up the greatest of all human freedoms, that freedom to think. The thing is, no one can take that freedom away from you no matter how hard they try, it is always given away freely.

Thinkers Know Why They Believe What They Believe

Back in the early 70's there was a time that I was thinking of becoming a Salvation Army officer. I was working full time at a corps in Vermont. I was a young Christian and still not sure of what God had in store for me. I served under Brigadier Thelma Basset, a lady in her seventies who had been with the Salvation Army most of her life. She would often question everything I had to say about my faith. Not that she did not agree with it or that I was wrong, it was that she wanted me to know why I believed the things I believed.

Brigadier Basset would want me to show her in Scripture why I believed something was true. She would question my decisions and make me give reasons for all I did. She drove me nuts! What Brigadier

Basset really did was teach me to think and to make sure I understood what I believed before I tried to convince other that they should believe. A habit I follow to this day. At the time Brigadier Basset drove me crazy, in the end, she was one of the best teachers I ever had in my life. I thank God for her to this day.

Have you ever asked yourself, why you believe what you believe? You may be surprised on how many people have not. One reason people avoid thinking about what they believe is because the result will cause them to act on it. Helen Keller once said, "People do not like to think. If one thinks, one must reach conclusions. Conclusions are not always pleasant." If I truly do believe that there is a right and wrong way we should live, then I have to be responsible to live by those rules. If I believe that all people have value and a purpose, then knowing why I believe that means I must treat all people as if they have value and a purpose. There is no neutral ground in life, no matter how much you or others try to make it so.

Thinkers Are Willing To Do The Work Of Thinking

Henry Ford famously said, "Thinking is the hardest work there is, which is probably the reason why so few engage in it." Thinking is hard work. Thinking is not sitting around letting any thought drift in and out of your mind. Thinking is action. Thinking is deliberate, purposeful and directed. You will find many great achievers throughout history, set time aside to think. They understood, - as success-minded people do - that thinking is a focused activity.

The work of thinking is the work of planning or strategy. It is knowing where you are going and thinking through how you will arrive at that destination. Every successful battle ever fought was won, not by might but by strategic thinking. Generals and leaders who took the time to plan out the attack and how the battle would be fought. Every great invention that has blessed the human race came from people who took the time to plan, work and plan some more to achieve the results they were looking for.

Thinkers are achievers. It is the ones who take the time to think through a problem or challenge who find the answers they need. Sadly, too many today are the victims of not thinking. They have no plan for their life and when the difficult times come - and they always come - they fall to the wave of events rather than create those events. There is an old saying that goes, "Most people spend more time planning their summer vacation then planning their lives." Success in any area of life does not just happen. It must be caused to happen and that only comes by thinking things through and doing what it takes to make things happen.

"You are today where your thoughts have brought you. You will be tomorrow where your thoughts take you." - James Allen

Thinkers Will Stand Alone

When you allow popular opinion and current trends to control your thinking you are not willing to take the risks of standing alone. Success-minded people who are willing to think on their own know that sometimes it means you must stand alone. Others may take the easy way out but you cannot. Just because the majority may think a certain way does not allow the thinker to do the same. They will think things through and come up with a sound and purposeful opinion. Author A.A. Milne, creator of Winnie-the-pooh, said, "The third-rate mind is only happy when it is thinking with the majority. The second-rate mind is only happy when it is thinking with the minority. The first-rate mind is only happy when it is thinking."

Without a doubt, the greatest destroyer of personal freedom in this country is found in the disguise of political correctness. Political correctness, by its very existence means that you can no longer think for yourself. You must think like everyone else, you must agree with everyone else, you must be like everyone else. Political correctness is the mindset of Orwell's 1984. So funny how we feared the book but embraced the reality.

I believe General Gorge S. Patton was right when he said, "If everyone is thinking alike, then someone isn't thinking." We do not think alike nor were we created to think alike. Successful people fight this evil and refuse to be just like everyone else. They know that there are those who will achieve more than others. There are those who will win and succeed. True freedom is not a guarantee that everyone will succeed in life, it is the guarantee that everyone will have the opportunity to succeed. That opportunity is just having the freedom to follow your dream and to be a thinker. Once you give the advantage to someone rather than allow them to create the advantage you rob from them the very power to be a success.

Thinkers Are Creative

Mr. Rogers was a well known children's TV personality for many years. He was the guiding light to over a generation of children with his gentle and welcoming manner. When the world of grown-ups would become fearful and turbulent, Mr. Rogers brought children understanding, peace and the knowledge that it would be okay. Children knew that Mr. Rogers believed in them and he could be trusted. He would often tell his young audience, "It is good to be curious. Curiosity plants seeds in the garden of your mind." Those seeds would grow and become great things.

Thinkers are curious by nature. They wonder the "what if" questions in life. These thinkers are the creative force that keeps us moving forward. It is not enough for them to think of what could be, that must make it be. The word impossible is not in their vocabulary, nor are words like quiet, give-up, can't be done and too much work. Discovering the unknown is in the air they breathe and they are the ones who change the world every day. When the cure for cancer, the answer to world hunger and the solution to the challenges we face comes, it will be by a success-minded thinker.

Thinkers know that we will never get anywhere in life if we surrender to common opinion and keep facing challenges with the same old thinking. Albert Einstein said, "We can't solve problems by using the same kind of thinking we used when we created them." have you ever noticed how many times those who are supposed to know better and have answers for the problems we face, just reuse the same answers they came up with before? I am far from a genius and yet even I can figure this one out.

If there was one gift that was in my power to give to every person in this country it would be the gift of curiosity. Curiosity did not kill the cat. Curiosity can create a cat. For those who possess a curious mind there are no limits to what they can achieve. Curiosity is not dependent on education (often, education kills curiosity - but that is another topic), on faith, money, position, class, family or any other factor. If you are in the human race you have the ability to be curious and that ability can catapulted you to wonders untold.

"The actions of men are the best interpreters of their thoughts." - John Locke

Since no one can take the ability to think from you, no one can give it to you either. You must build it in yourself. Do as Mr. Rogers says and plant seeds in the garden of your mind. The late Zig Ziglar always said, "You were born to win and have the seeds of greatness in you." I believe with all that is in me that is true. I have seen it over and over again in the lives of people who discovered their ability to think on their own. Once the questions start, there is no end to it. Never fear the thinking person. Truth is always truth and for the one who thinks, they will find that truth and it will set them free.

CONCLUSION

A model is an abstraction or simplification of a system. Models can assume many different forms—from a model volcano in a high school science fair to a sophisticated astrophysical model simulated using a supercomputer. Models are simplified representations of a part of reality that we want to learn more about. George Box stated:, "Essentially, all models are wrong, but some are useful." They are wrong because they are simplifications, and they can be useful because we can learn from them.

A mental model is a model that is constructed and simulated within a conscious mind. To be "conscious" is to be aware of the world around you and yourself in relation to the world. Let's take a moment to think about how this process works operationally.

Thinking About Systems

The human mind is very good at simulating mental models of our immediate physical reality. Things get harder when we start thinking about abstract systems.

A market is a good example of an abstract system. In a market system, price acts as a signal of aggregate demand for a commodity. You can't "see" a market like you can "see" a tree in front of you. A market does not exist in a particular physical location. A market is an abstract concept that exists in the collective minds of all who participate in it. Even though markets do not exist physically, they have an enormous impact on our lives nonetheless.

When the global economic crisis hit, people started saving money instead of spending it. Retailers in turn dropped prices to boost consumer spending. But when consumers saw prices dropping rapidly, they delayed purchases in the hope of achieving additional savings—leading to a price deflation loop.

When the global economic crisis hit in late 2008, retailers began to struggle financially because consumer purchases declined rapidly. People were worried about the economy and started saving money instead of spending it. This started happening just before the holiday shopping season—a make-or break period for many retailers. So, in an effort to boost demand, retailers began dropping prices.

This process led to price deflation, because consumers saw prices dropping rapidly and began delaying purchases as a result. The outcome of simulating their mental models of the market informed their decision making: "I should wait to buy this because the price keeps dropping."

This mental model paints a pretty picture for consumers over the short term: low prices in a down economy. As the deflationary dynamics play out over the long term, however, the picture becomes bleak. As prices spin downward, profits decline, and businesses are forced to lay off workers or close up shop entirely. As unemployment increases, consumers' perception of the stability of the economy decreases, and they spend even less (see "Economic Stability Loop").

Economists and policy makers use sophisticated computer models to help them understand markets. Consumers, on the other hand, use simple mental models when making purchasing decisions. The more sophisticated models inform policy makers of the long-term consequences of consumers' reduction in spending, so they react by trying to jump-start spending with stimulus programs. In the U. S., we've seen a few of these programs during 2009: the "Cash for Clunkers" rebate program, the first-time home buyer tax credit, and the social security payroll tax cut.

As the deflationary dynamics play out over the long term, the picture becomes bleak. As prices spin downward, profits decline and businesses are forced to lay off workers or close up shop entirely. As unemployment increases, consumers' perception of the stability of the economy decreases and they spend even less.

Complex Systems

Often, it is hard for us to define the optimal boundaries for a mental model. We tend to have a narrow focus and act on short-term dynamics within our mental models. For example, in the model above, our understanding changes when we expand the boundaries to include profits and layoffs.

However, we are generally not very good at mentally simulating complex systems with interdependencies, lots of variables, and delays. This is where software steps in. Using systems thinking software, we can transform our mental models into operational models that we can simulate more reliably using a computer. Doing so not only helps us create new knowledge and understanding, but also helps us construct better mental models in the future.

www.ingramcontent.com/pod-product-compliance
Lightning Source LLC
Chambersburg PA
CBHW060421290526
45791CB00002B/844